INCREASE YOUR INFLUENCE AT WORK

Perry McIntosh
and Richard A. Luecke

AMACOM

AMERICAN MANAGEMENT ASSOCIATION

New York • Atlanta • Brussels • Chicago • Mexico City • San Francisco
Shanghai • Tokyo • Toronto • Washington, D.C.

Library of Congress Cataloging-in-Publication Data

McIntosh, Perry.
    Increase your influence at work / Perry McIntosh and Richard A. Luecke.
        p.   cm.
    Includes index.
    ISBN-13: 978-0-8144-1601-3 (pbk.)
    ISBN-10: 0-8144-1601-2 (pbk.)
        1. Success in business.   2. Influence (Psychology)   3. Assertiveness (Psychology)   4. Interpersonal communication.   I. Luecke, Richard. II. Title.
    HF5386.M4748 2011
    650.1'3—dc22

                                                                    2010006515

About AMA

American Management Association (www.amanet.org) is a world leader in talent development, advancing the skills of individuals to drive business success. Our mission is to support the goals of individuals and organizations through a complete range of products and services, including classroom and virtual seminars, webcasts, webinars, podcasts, conferences, corporate and government solutions, business books, and research. AMA's approach to improving performance combines experiential learning—learning through doing—with opportunities for ongoing professional growth at every step of one's career journey.

Printing number

10   9   8   7   6   5   4   3   2   1

CONTENTS

PREFACE

This book is about influence, how you can develop it, and how you can use it to affect the behavior or thinking of people with whom you work. The ability to influence others is an important ingredient of success for people at every level in an organization, including nonmanagers. Even those who have formal organizational power benefit from understanding and using influence at work. Every newly minted manager quickly discovers that formal power is overrated as a tool for getting things done. Managers' authority is constrained by dependence on others and by the necessities of "participative" management. It's getting harder and harder to order subordinates around! And the cooperation of peers and other groups cannot be gained through compulsion.

People who know how to influence enjoy many benefits. They can:

➤ Lead and manage more effectively

➤ Frame important issues their way

➤ Win support for their ideas and projects

➤ Contribute more fully to important decisions

➤ Resolve conflicts more easily

➤ Advance their careers

More important, they have a greater measure of control over their lives at work. Instead of being passive participants and simply doing what they're told, they have a greater say in how the scripts of their working lives are written. And that is worth a lot in terms of work-life satisfaction.

Whether you're a supervisor, a manager, or an individual contributor, you can increase your influence at work. And this book will show you how. The first chapter explains the concept of influence and how it differs from those other tools for getting things done: power and persuasion. The next two chapters present a conceptual framework with two main elements: (1) the foundation attributes of influence (trustworthiness, reliability, and assertiveness), and (2) six practical tactics for influencing others. Because influence is based on trust, the foundation attributes are things you *must exhibit* if you aim to alter the thinking and behavior of others at work. Once you have those attributes, you can select and apply the tactics most appropriate for your situation.

In Chapters 4 and 5 you'll discover where the rubber meets the road. These chapters offer practical tips for influencing the three most important sets of people in life at work: your subordinates; your peers; and *numero uno*, your boss.

Finally, there's the issue of ethics. Influence has a potential dark side. It can be—and has been—used for the wrong purposes: to deceive, to manipulate, and to further selfish ends at the expense of the general good. Our final chapter examines these ethical issues in terms of the influencer's ends and means.

That's it in a nutshell. So read on and learn how you can become more influential at work.

CHAPTER 1

INFLUENCE, POWER, AND PERSUASION

"Our new general manager has had a positive influence on our
business culture."

"It's clear that Helen was much influenced by her mentor."

"Our state senator was nabbed for influence peddling in an FBI
sting operation."

"Although Steve is the leader of a cross-functional team, he
seems to have very little influence over his team members."

The term *influence* is used often, and in all facets of life. But
what does it really mean, especially in a workplace context?
And how does it differ from related concepts, such as power
and persuasion? This chapter answers these questions and sets the
stage for a greater understanding of influence and how you can
develop and apply it at work.

Power, influence, and persuasion have one thing in common:
Each is something we use to get what we want from others—a tan-
gible item, a particular behavior (or change in behavior), or accep-

tance of our ideas or modes of thinking. Let's consider each of these concepts in turn.

POWER

Power is the ability to get what we want by virtue of command or compulsion. In the workplace, people who occupy certain positions—as executives, managers, and supervisors—are invested with some level of power. They are authorized by the organization within certain limits to give orders, allocate or withhold resources, and make decisions. Thus, your boss has the power (again, within certain limits) to make decisions on who will be hired and promoted and how work will be done. For example, it's likely that your boss has the power to determine when you and other subordinates will take vacation days. When the CEO tells the head of manufacturing, "I want costs reduced by 10 percent over the next six months—show me how you are going to do it," she's not *asking* the department head to do something. She's not trying to influence or persuade him. Instead, she's using her power of position to command or compel a particular behavior.

Most people in Western societies have a visceral distrust of power and power differences between people; they favor equality between people. They are uncomfortable with the idea that some individuals can command or compel others. To them, power harkens to historical conditions in which one party arbitrarily exercised his or her will over others. This discomfort with power spills over into the modern workplace, where people can be less responsive to direct orders than to a manager's appeals for their cooperation. Thus, new managers quickly discover that their positional power doesn't get them very far; bossing people around is very unproductive. These managers may have the power to command certain actions, and their subordinates may be obliged to obey, but compulsion seldom enlists a person's best efforts. If anything, it may produce resistance. If the work must be done quickly and well, managers find that appeals for collaboration are generally more productive than compulsion.

This is not so say that power has no place in organizations. Power is, in fact, essential in organizational life. Let's look at some situations when the use of positional power is necessary to get things done:

➤ **When a Crisis Occurs.** Crises almost always demand a rapid and unequivocal response. People look to a leader who commands them to get out when the building is on fire. There is no time for discussion, convincing, and consensus building. What is needed to handle a crisis is a command response, not participative management or employee empowerment. Employees recognize this and generally accept the commands of leaders during periods of crisis.

➤ **When Consensus Cannot Be Reached.** Key decisions can sometimes be made by consensus, but when people fail to reach consensus a manager must use positional power to break the deadlock and make a decision that allows the group to move forward.

➤ **When Subordinates Lack Essential Skills or Experience.** Exercising power may make sense in some situations, but not in others. For example, a manager who tries to boss around technical professionals or other highly skilled employees does so at his peril. Skillful people who are dedicated to their work expect to work *with* their bosses in getting things done; they do not respond well to commands or compulsion. Successful managers of these employees can command the "what" but not the "how"—they can insist on certain results but leave it to skilled employees to determine how the results are accomplished. However, the opposite may be true of employees who are new to their jobs or who lack important skills. In these cases, close direction and command may be appropriate.

➤ **When Employees Lack Key Information.** Whether for reasons of legality, confidentiality, or organizational complexity, sometimes only the manager can have access to the "big picture."

➤ **When the Buck Stops Here.** Although it is wise to get input from others on many difficult decisions, managers must take ultimate responsibility for some decisions, such as the decision to hire or terminate an employee.

INFLUENCE

Influence is a means of getting what we want *without* command or compulsion. Unlike power, which can be exercised only by certain people such as managers and executives by virtue of their positions, influence can be exercised by anyone at any level of the organization. For example, a savvy manager who enjoys the power of position sees the wisdom of not exercising it. To return to the example of the vacation schedule, a "decree from on high" that no staff may take a vacation during July would likely engender resentment; the department might experience a rash of unfortunate "illnesses" that month. The savvy manager recognizes that she'll get more of what she wants by applying influence. Explaining her concerns and asking for cooperation to meet department needs will probably be more effective. For her, influence is a "soft" form of power.

In contrast to his manager, an engineer working in a research and development lab may have no formal power; nevertheless, he may have substantial influence over both his boss and his peers if he possesses uncanny creativity and problem-solving abilities that they recognize and appreciate. When he speaks, other people listen—and they often willingly adopt his point of view. For him, too, influence is a form of soft power.

PERSUASION

What about *persuasion*, a term often found in guides for success in the new "flat" workplace? Persuasion is another way of getting what we want without command or compulsion. Persuasion, however, is not influence per se, merely a tool. Persuasion involves the use of rhetorical devices such as logical argument and emotional appeals. Both those who have positional power and those who do not can utilize persuasion. Consider this example:

> Fran, a midlevel financial analyst, is having lunch with other employees of his department. None has a reporting relationship with anyone else at the table. As their discussion turns from sports to work, Fran offers his view on the company's bank line of credit, which he sees as a problem.
>
> "I've studied the sales forecast for next year," he tells them, "and our current $1 million credit line, when added to our projected working capital, won't be enough to finance the production and inventory we'll need to fill those forecasted sales. If we can't talk the bank into expanding our line of credit—say to $2 million—we may end up with thousands of unit orders that we cannot fill. If that happens, heads will roll."

He then goes on to explain how he arrived at the $2 million figure and how they might get the bank to give it to them.

In this example, Fran is applying persuasive communication with the goal of influencing the thinking of his peers about an important business matter. And because he is interested in the success of the company, we'd expect that Fran would direct the same line of persuasion communication to his boss, the CFO:

"I've gone over the numbers several times," Fran tells the CFO in a meeting later that week, "and it seems clear that we'll need close to $2 million in additional cash in order to support this fall's anticipated sales orders. A larger bank line of credit would be the easiest and least costly way to provide that financing. I have all of my analysis on a spreadsheet. Would you like to see it?"

Persuasion is a form of communication that enlists logical or emotional appeals—or both—in order to get certain things or to affect the beliefs and behaviors of others. Though persuasion is popularly associated with advertisers and salespeople, almost everyone in an organization from top to bottom employs persuasion at one time or another. For example:

➤ A CEO tries to persuade the board of directors that a change in company strategy is necessary.

➤ The general manager of a manufacturing unit engages in persuasive communication with her functional managers and staff, hoping that they will adopt her enthusiasm for a new program of quality control.

➤ A staff person tries to persuade his boss to invest in new software that will make people in the office more productive.

➤ A department manager persuades a peer that her participation in a joint effort will benefit both departments.

In getting what we want from others, persuasion is a tool that we all reach for with great frequency. If you stop and think about it, you can probably identify daily instances in which you have been on either the giving or receiving end of persuasion, both at work and at home.

PUTTING IT ALL TOGETHER

Do you see how the three related concepts introduced in this chapter—power, influence, and persuasion—fit together? If you don't, the graphic model depicted in Figure 1-1 will give you a clearer

FIGURE 1-1. POWER, INFLUENCE, AND PERSUASION.

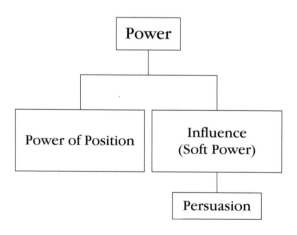

picture. Note that influence, like the power of position, is a form of power. It is aided by the tool of persuasion. Both forms of power aim for the same thing—to get what we want from others—although through different means.

CHAPTER REVIEW

To review what you have learned, take the following open-book review quiz.

1. Power was defined here as the ability to get what we want by virtue of command or compulsion. Describe one example of the effective exercise of power in your workplace by you or by someone else.

_____

_____

_____

_____

2. *Influence* was defined as a means of getting what we want *without* command or compulsion. Describe one occasion in which you successfully exercised influence. What was the result?

_____

_____

_____

_____

3. Describe one situation in your workplace in which the use of influence would be more appropriate and effective than the application of formal power—that is, ordering someone to do something.

_____

_____

_____

_____

4. Persuasion is a tool of influence. Recollect and describe a recent in-stance in which someone at work tried to persuade you to do what he or she wished.

_____

_____

_____

_____

CHAPTER 2

THE FOUNDATION OF INFLUENCE

N ow that you understand the meaning of influence and the related concepts of power and persuasion, we can move on to practical steps you can take to enhance your influence at work. Conceptually, it's useful to think of influence in terms of a structure built on a solid foundation of personal attributes and supportive tactics, as shown in Figure 2-1. The attributes are trustworthiness, reliability, and assertiveness. These are personal attributes you can develop over time and are the subjects of this chapter. Think of them as the "ante" the would-be influencer must pay to join the game. In and of themselves these attributes will not give you substantial influence, but you cannot be highly influential without them. To win the game, you must employ one or more supporting tactics; you'll learn about those in Chapter 3.

FIGURE 2-1. THE STRUCTURE OF INFLUENCE.

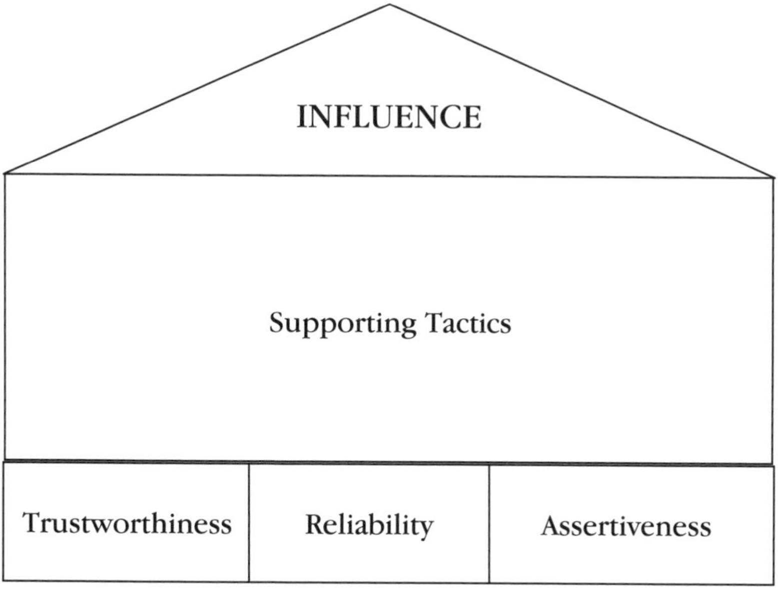

TRUSTWORTHINESS

It's obvious that a person considered untrustworthy will have a hard time influencing the decisions, behavior, or thinking of others. This example makes it clear why:

> Last year Jane lobbied heavily on behalf of a plan to create and staff a new sales territory in the Minnesota-Wisconsin area. "It should be profitable within two years," she insisted. People were interested because top management was pushing for profit growth, and her plan supported that important goal. The national sales manager became very excited and began talking up Jane's plan to his boss, the vice president of sales and marketing. "Opening a small office in Madison, Wisconsin, with

three outside salespeople could contribute $2 million to corporate profitability if Jane is right," he told his boss.

Interest in the plan evaporated, however, once it became clear that Jane hadn't taken the trouble to develop realistic cost estimates for the expansion. They were simply off-the-top-of-her-head guesses. Worse, her anticipated sales revenues from the new territory were based on what everyone considered to be unrealistic assumptions. The national sales manager was embarrassed by his initial enthusiasm, which had reduced his credibility with his own boss. Consequently, the next time Jane tried to promote a new idea, she was ignored.

Jane is a fictitious character, but her behavior is drawn from that of people we've all met in the workplace at one time or another. These are not bad people; they often have the best of intentions. Unfortunately, their suggestions cannot be accepted at face value because they don't go to the trouble of checking their facts and building a solid, supportable case. They fail the test of trustworthiness, with the result that they have little influence on others.

Consider what would happen if Jane had approached her case for an expansion into the Minnesota-Wisconsin area in a very different, more credible way—not off the top of her head, but based on solid facts, analysis, and realistic assumptions. The risks in the plan would have been identified, and where critical information was lacking she would have said something like this: "At this point I cannot offer a revenue estimate for the proposed new territory. We do *not* know the total demand for our products in that region, or how much of it our competitors are now getting. That information must be obtained through market research before we invest in the idea. I've begun talking with our market research staff about how we can get those data."

Who would you find more worthy of trust, the new Jane or the old Jane? Who would have greater influence over you? The next time Jane makes a suggestion, would you be inclined to believe that she had done her homework?

In a business context, trust is something that's earned *over time* by:

> ➤ Telling the truth, no matter now painful
> ➤ Delivering both the good news and the bad
> ➤ Taking responsibility for our mistakes
> ➤ Identifying the upside *and* downside potential of our suggestions
> ➤ Recognizing the value of ideas that compete with our own
> ➤ Giving careful thought and analysis to our proposals
> ➤ Providing decision makers with the information they need to make wise choices
> ➤ Putting organizational goals above our own
> ➤ Respecting confidentiality
> ➤ Having the courage to say, "I don't know" when appropriate

The cumulative effects of these behaviors over time invest a person with the trustworthiness that makes influence possible.

Which of your workplace colleagues are trustworthy? Which are not? How do the people you work with rate your trustworthiness?

RELIABILITY

In the workplace, reliability is a personal quality that gives others confidence in saying or thinking, "I can count on that person to follow through." Not everyone has a reputation for reliability;

those who lack it have little ability to influence others, as the following example demonstrates:

> Harold is a bundle of energy and ideas. Just about everyone he works with initially finds his enthusiasm and upbeat attitude infectious. His plan for reengineering the customer service process, for example, gets people very excited. "We can do more for our customers, and do it faster and cheaper," he says, "if we examine what we are doing and think of creative ways to generate more value at a lower cost." It's a great idea and everyone buys into it. It also aligns nicely with the company's cost-saving initiative. Management gives Harold the go-ahead to organize a process reengineering team and work with it to map out a better, faster, cheaper way to deliver customer service.
>
> Unfortunately, Harold is long on ideas and short on follow-through. After two months, his team hasn't gotten organized or developed a plan for reaching its goal. Harold is now talking to management about another way of improving the business.

Everyone loves upbeat, optimistic employees. But we don't take them seriously if they, like Harold, don't complete their assignments or follow through on their ideas. From management's perspective, there are A players and then there are all the rest. The A players are the people who do what they say and get the job done. When they speak, management listens because these individuals have *earned* the right to be heard and to have influence. Harold could have been an A player because he had an idea that aligned with the goals of management. But because he didn't execute his idea, he lost his opportunity to be influential. Unless he changes the way he operates, he will be consigned to the netherworld of B- and C-level employees—people who lack influence with management.

Like trust, a reputation for reliability is developed *over time*. Start developing yours today by:

- ➢ Never making promises you cannot or will not keep
- ➢ Remembering that decisions are ineffective in the absence of implementation (follow-through)
- ➢ Not giving up when you encounter impediments
- ➢ Keeping all your agreements, large and small (this includes being on time for appointments and meetings)
- ➢ Doing your research

ASSERTIVENESS

Assertiveness is another foundation attribute of influential people. You will exercise little influence if you allow others to push you aside, or if you simply keep your light under a basket.

Assertiveness is a mode of personal behavior and communication characterized by a willingness to stand up for one's needs and interests in an open and direct way. The assertive person stands up for things that matter to him while respecting the things that matter to others. You've surely known people who fit this description:

- ➢ The boss who is open to your ideas, but who reserves the right to make final decisions
- ➢ The coworker who isn't afraid to speak up during meetings and to defend her viewpoints

People who function in the *assertive* mode have a strong sense of self-esteem that allows them to protect their needs and interests and advance their agendas. They use open, direct, and honest communication with others. They make themselves visible in organizations and work collaboratively with others. They take responsibility for their decisions and behavior, and own up to their mistakes. They're calculated-risk takers.

Assertiveness is best understood in relation to two very different and opposing forms of personal behavior and communication: passivity and aggression (see Figure 2-2).

FIGURE 2-2. THE CONTINUUM OF PERSONAL BEHAVIOR AND COMMUNICATION.

Passive	Assertive	Aggressive
• Does not stand up for one's interests and viewpoints but submits to those of others • Does not share one's views on what's important • Allows others to disrespect one's opinions and rights • Does not try to influence others • Demonstrates lack of confidence in dealing with others	• Uses direct communication; doesn't beat around the bush • Makes one's agenda clear • Is not afraid to attempt to influence others • Respects views and rights of others • Defends one's views, rights, and boundaries against infringement • Controls anger • Uses aggressive behavior defensively • Is open to influence even when seeking to influence others	• Aims for dominance over others • Imposes one's views on others • Does not respect views or boundaries of others • Is resistant to influence by others • May lose control of anger • Uses threats to get one's way • Is "in your face" • Aims to be highly visible

Passivity

Passivity is an unassertive condition characterized by submissiveness and a fear or unwillingness to stand up for one's needs and interests. The passive person holds back from attempting to influence others and instead allows others to influence him and disrespect his rights and boundaries. Because the passive person does not assert his views or argue on their behalf, his views are generally unknown to others, making dialogue and idea sharing difficult.

People who function in the passive mode are likely to put the needs and concerns of others ahead of their own. They're inclined to be quiet, soft-spoken, and even timid. They prefer to be invisible and find it difficult to speak up in meetings or speak out about things that upset them. Rather than confront a problematic person or situation directly, they will hold their feelings inside or complain about the problem to someone else. When they feel angry, they're apt to suppress it.

Are you a passive person at work—out of either disinterest, fear, or lack of confidence? Do you know others who demonstrate the characteristics of passivity—perhaps a colleague who seldom speaks up during meetings or when decisions that affect him are being made, or perhaps a subordinate who is reluctant to share his ideas with you?

Aggression

As a form of personal behavior or communication, *aggression* is the opposite of passivity. The aggressive person has no reluctance in imposing his views on others, or harming their interests in the pursuit of his own. Rather than collaborating with others, the aggressive person prefers to dominate them, using threats, organizational authority, or bullying when necessary. He tends to micromanage the work of subordinates; things must be done his way. This person resists the influence of those seen as less powerful. In many cases, the aggressive person is unaware of his effect on others—he thinks that he's simply being assertive. Consider this example:

> I just got a 360-degree performance review from my staff, boss, and peers. They said that I seem obsessed with micromanaging the department. My direct reports claimed that they have little input into decisions and that I look for someone to blame when things go wrong. They claimed that I use my power to belittle them. Someone even used the word *toxic* to describe me. Toxic! Where did that come from? I don't see myself that way. I push my staff to perform at a peak level, as any good manager would. Hey, my bonus depends on those numbers—and so do their bonuses. Even so, our numbers have been down for the last two quarters. My boss thinks there's a link between my style and those disappointing results.

People who function in the aggressive mode look after their own needs and interests first. The needs and interests of others are always secondary. Reminiscent of the old Soviet line, "What's mine is mine, what's yours is negotiable," they stand up for their rights, but often at the expense of others.

Aggressive people are often loud and visible in organizations. They have difficulty controlling their anger and may humiliate others in public. They violate other people's boundaries. Indirect forms of aggression, such as sarcasm, are used to put down or control others.

. . . .

You can probably see the superiority of the assertive mode of behavior and communication over passivity and aggression—from both a personal career and an organizational effectiveness perspective. By being open to influence, the assertive person is able to influence others in return. By defending her views and rights from infringement, she makes coworkers recognize that she must be taken seriously and approached with respect. By speaking her mind on issues that matter to her and to the organization, she contributes to important decisions, thus influencing the future direction of the enterprise. Higher management, peers, and subordinates alike see the assertive individual as a person to be reckoned with—a person who has something to contribute. This often translates into greater influence and career opportunities.

In contrast, the passive person is like a leaf floating in a stream, drawn along by the current, making no impact on its direction or speed. He will have few opportunities for advancement. For his part, the aggressive person creates problems for the organization and for those around him. While aggression may get him what he wants in many cases, that behavior will prove costly in the long run. Coworkers whose views and insights are disrespected will stop offering them. Peers whose rights are infringed will become enemies and may actively undermine him. When the office bully makes a serious mistake or gets into a tough situation, no one will come to his aid.

Where do you fall in the continuum described in Figure 2-2? Are you generally passive, assertive, or aggressive? If you're not near the center of this continuum, use the descriptive bullet points in the center column as models for your future behavior and communication style at work.

Effective and assertive verbal messages are delivered through brief, declarative sentences that are specific, concrete, and to the point. People who use direct communication don't waltz around their main point, ramble, hesitate, hedge their statements, excuse themselves, or do anything else that prolongs or confuses their messages. Consider each of the following examples of unassertive speech and their assertive equivalents:

UNASSERTIVE	ASSERTIVE
➤ Perhaps, if you don't mind—and I realize the subject may seem a bit arcane—but if you're open to it, we might look at another approach to financing this phase of our expansion.	➤ There's another approach to financing this phase of our expansion. I recommend that we do a sale-leaseback. Here's how it works. . . .
➤ Oh, excuse me, Doug, I'm sorry to bother you when you're so busy, but, ah, I was wondering, and maybe this isn't the time, but I was wondering if I could talk with you sometime about my vacation schedule. Is that possible?	➤ Doug, I'd like to talk with you about my vacation schedule. Can we meet next week?

Note how the unassertive communicator beats around the bush and qualifies what he hopes to say ("If you're open to

it") and seems to be apologizing ("Excuse me"; "I'm sorry").
Meaning is lost in a blather of hemming and hawing. The assertive speaker, in contrast, uses simple declarative sentences
("There's another approach") and is commanding in nature
("I recommend that . . ."). Try following similar assertive approaches on a regular basis. As you craft short, clear, concrete
sentences that precisely convey your meaning, you'll hear and
feel yourself becoming more assertive.

. . . .

◆ ◆ ◆ ◆ ◆

Trustworthiness. Reliability. Assertiveness. When you practice these
attributes, you will begin to develop a positive reputation and have
a solid foundation for personal influence at work. But remember,
influence is a work in progress—it's easy to tear down this foundation by acting in untrustworthy or unreliable ways. And even when
you have the foundation firmly in place, to be truly effective, you'll
need to go a step further. Our next chapter tells you how.

CHAPTER REVIEW

To review what you have learned, take the following open-book
review quiz.

1. What are the three foundation attributes of influence?

_____

_____

_____

_____

2. Describe three things you can do to be viewed by others as trustworthy.

_____

_____

_____

_____

3. Describe three things you can do to establish a reputation for reliability.

_____

_____

_____

4. Explain what is meant by each of the following behaviors in the workplace context:

Passive

_____

_____

_____

_____

Aggressive

_____

_____

_____

_____

Assertive

_____

_____

_____

_____

CHAPTER 3

TACTICS

———————

The previous chapter described the foundation attributes on which influence is built: trustworthiness, reliability, and an assertive style of behavior and communication. Think of these as prerequisites—as personal characteristics you must bring to the table if you really want to get into the influence game. But once you're in the game, what then? What tactics can you employ to influence other people in your organization? This is the question we will answer in this chapter.

Figure 3-1 revisits the "structure of influence" concept introduced in Chapter 2, adding six supporting tactics onto its foundation of personal attributes:

1. Create reciprocal credits.
2. Be a source of expertise, information, and resources.
3. Help people find common ground.
4. Frame issues your way.

5. Build a network of support.

6. Employ persuasive communication.

Although this list of tactics is not complete, it includes those available to all readers. These are actions that anyone in any organization can take to increase his or her influence.

CREATE RECIPROCAL CREDITS

Every society we know of honors the *principle of reciprocity*. According to this principle, if you do a favor for someone, that person owes you a favor in return—and you have a right to expect it. Until

FIGURE 3-1. THE STRUCTURE OF INFLUENCE WITH ITS SUPPORTING TACTICS.

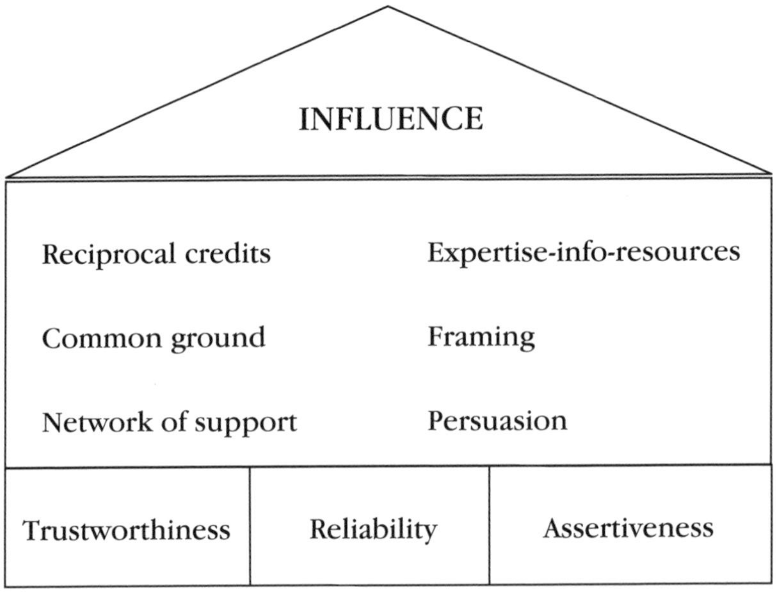

that favor is returned, you have a "credit" on the balance sheet of your relationship with that other person. You might think of it as an "account receivable"—a value owed to you by someone else.

This principle of reciprocity operates in all sectors of human affairs. Consider the world of politics. In the United States, most organized interest groups—from corn growers to bankers to teachers' unions to green energy producers—have lobbyists in the nation's capital. These lobbyists have a common goal: to influence legislation and policy in favor of their organizations or clients. Contributing to reelection campaigns is one method used to gain influence. According to the Center for Responsive Politics, the nation's 15,138 registered lobbyists made political contributions of $3.24 billion in 2008. That's well over $5 million, on average, for every senator and congressional representative in Washington.

Those contributions aim to support the reelection of politicians friendly to the interests of lobbying organizations. However, for recipients, those contributions create a sense of obligation to *reciprocate* in some way, such as giving contributing lobbyists opportunities to be heard on legislative matters that affect their clients' interests. As the old saying goes, he who pays the piper calls the tune. And there's plenty of evidence that contributors of campaign funds *do* receive the access they seek.

Reciprocity operates in the workplace as well. Because his boss was under pressure to make a presentation to top management on Wednesday, Chuck spent part of his weekend developing her PowerPoint slides. Credit Chuck's account; his boss owes him. Meanwhile, Chuck has asked the IT manager to fix a problem with his PC. That's the IT manager's job, but because that manager knocked herself out to solve the problem right away, Chuck owes her something in return. Add that to Chuck's accounts payable.

In their excellent book *Influence Without Authority*, Allan

Cohen and David Bradford note that "exchanges" like the ones just described are commonplace in organizational life.[1] These exchanges occur between peers, between bosses and their subordinates, and between company employees and outsiders such as customers and suppliers. These exchanges may involve money, services, resources, or information. And every exchange represents an opportunity to create influence.

Take a moment to think about and write down the reciprocal credits owed to you, and those you owe to others. Who are your leading creditors and debtors? The principle of reciprocity provides you with opportunities to create influence if you use them tactically. The following sections provide suggestions for making the most of those opportunities.

Identify the People You Wish to Influence

You have only so many favors to do and resources to share, so identify the people you most want to influence—the people who can help you to be successful at work. Though it's good policy to be openhanded with everyone, scarcity of time and resources demands that you prioritize your efforts.

Determine What They Value

The principle of reciprocity works only when the favor you do for someone, or the resource you share, is truly valued by the other party. In our previous example, how much does the boss value the PowerPoint slides Chuck created for her over the weekend? Well, if they made her look good to top management, we can assume that the boss attached a high value to Chuck's slides. You get the idea.

Make a conscious effort to determine what people value. In most cases, people put a high value on anything that will do the following:

> ➢ Make their work easier and better—for example, a particular piece of equipment or software, or instruction on how to make better use of the resources they have

> ➢ Help them achieve their goals—for example, providing resources to a team effort or taking over some mundane task so that a coworker can concentrate on a key goal

> ➢ Make them feel appreciated—for example, an occasional pat on the back or praise in front of their peers (neither of which costs you anything)

Stop for a moment and think about the people you most want to influence at work. What is within your power to share or contribute that these individuals would value highly? What would be the cost to you of providing these favors? We'll get more specific about these in our next chapter, which explains how to influence your subordinates, peers, and your boss.

If you're serious about becoming more influential, map out a systematic and long-term campaign for building credits in your account. Consider using a simple worksheet like the one shown in Figure 3-2. List the people on whom you'd like to have greater influence, and for each jot down one or two things you could actually do to help them succeed in their work. Then begin working your way through the list, adding to it as you learn more.

. . . .

You can increase your influence potential by systematically building up your stash of credits. Then, when you need sup-

FIGURE 3-2. WORKSHEET FOR BUILDING CREDITS.

People I'd like to influence	What I can do to make them more effective, successful, or appreciated
Herb/Advertising	Help Herb and his team to improve the Spring–Summer sales catalogue campaign by speeding up development of the new customer database.
Arlene/Sales Support	Delegate Carol to help Arlene's sales support group during the peak sales period (early July).
Leslie/Benefits Administration	Volunteer to join the task force she's leading to investigate alternative health benefit plans. Offer to conduct a financial analysis of each alternative.

port in getting something that *you* need, or when you want people to adopt your perspective, you can call in some of those IOUs. Not everyone will come through, but most will reciprocate out of a sense of fair play and their desire to keep you on board as one of their supporters. This tactic takes time to bear fruit, so begin today.

. . . .

BE A SOURCE OF EXPERTISE, INFORMATION, AND RESOURCES

Even if you lack organizational power, you can also gain and exercise influence if you become a source of valuable technical expertise, key information, or essential resources. Let's look at an example:

Romeo is a classic computer nerd. For the past six months he has been up to his eyeballs in a $10 million project to install the company's new enterprise software system—the kind of system that runs everything from order fulfillment to inventory control to accounting. No one really understands the details of the new system as well as Romeo, not even his boss, the vice president of technology. Consequently, when this VP meets with the top management team to discuss the project's progress, he brings Romeo along. When tough questions are asked, everyone turns to Romeo for the answers.

Romeo has no formal authority in the organization, but when technology issues are on the table, people at the top look to him for evaluations, insights, and advice.

In this example, Romeo has influence in one area of company operations because he has something that the people with power desperately need but do not have: technical expertise. They rely on him and value his opinions. If Romeo has attended to the foundation attributes, he may be able to parlay this limited influence into a broader influential "footprint."

Control of *key information and resources* likewise creates a potential to acquire and apply influence. Have you heard the term "go-to guy?" Do you have a go-to guy (or gal) in your organization? One of the authors recalls working with a private college that was very troubled by the low level of donations it received from alumni. Both trustees and administrators of the college wondered why their alumni contributions were so low relative to those of similar institutions. "Did our graduates leave with a low regard for our curriculum or faculty?" one administrator wondered aloud. "Did they have a bad experience with campus life?" asked another.

One staff person at the college had the information they needed to answer those questions and gain insights into alumni giving. As a long-term employee, this staff person had measured student satisfaction levels over many years. She had designed and administered satisfaction surveys to all graduating seniors for eight years in succession. Furthermore, she, more than anyone else, could draw clear interpretations from that deep pile of statistical data. She was, in effect, the "go-to gal" on alumni attitudes toward the college. And this gave her substantial influence with the administration.

. . . .

Do you have expertise that your company badly needs? Are you a "go-to person" with respect to key information? Do you control a resource that others need to succeed in their work? If you answered no to these questions, give some thought as to how you could build expertise in some area of importance to the company. Likewise, if you see an opportunity to gain control of information or resources that others need and value, go for it.

. . . .

HELP PEOPLE FIND COMMON GROUND

In their landmark book, *In Search of Excellence*, Tom Peters and Robert Waterman quoted a Motorola executive whose experience told him never to allow the company's plants to grow beyond one thousand employees. "Something just seems to go wrong when you get more people under one roof."[2] "Going wrong" can take many forms in large organizations: poor communication, misaligned efforts, lack of coordination, and so forth. These problems are experienced less frequently in small operations where people work in close proximity under the direction of a visible leader who articulates organizational goals clearly and often.

One of the greatest afflictions experienced by large organizations is silo mentality. Because specialization is needed, most employees of large organizations work within distinct functional units (silos), where they develop specialized skills and outlooks and focus on narrow goals. In the worst cases, people become so insular that they lose sight of the organization's goals and substitute self-interest in their place. Turf warfare follows as self-aggrandizing silo managers, like medieval barons, struggle with each other and with corporate headquarters for control of resources. Individual employees identify more strongly with their silo clan members than with other members of the corporation.

This unsatisfactory situation creates an opportunity for influential individuals who can help conflicting parties rise above their differences and parochial interests and find common ground. Consider the following example:

A company we'll call Gemini Company was a major U.S. publisher of college-level business, math, and science textbooks. It also had a trade book division that published in the areas of current events, history, science, and technology. Though these divisions shared the same corporate back office functions, they operated independently of one another. Each focused on its unique market, and each had its own sales and marketing operation. Their cultures were also very different. The textbook people operated in a static environment in which customers, potential authors, and competitors were clearly identified, and in which the subject matter changed slowly. The trade book people, in contrast, operated in a dynamic environment of fast-changing reader interests. The next "big book" could come from anywhere, and its success would be driven by its newsworthiness, reviews in the media, and the author's public visibility.

The two divisions generally coexisted peacefully under the same corporate roof, though neither held the other in high regard. The textbook people complained of their trade colleagues, "Their books generate all the publicity, but ours generate most of the profits." The trade book people, for their part, viewed their brethren on the other side of the building as dull plodders in a formulaic industry.

Opportunities for synergy between these two different divisions were few. Then suddenly they found themselves courting the same author, an eminent academic climatologist. The textbook people were offering him a lucrative contract to write a highly academic college textbook on weather and climate change, while editors in the trade division were asking him to pen a high-impact book on the global warming crisis. Gemini's CFO was alarmed when he discovered that the two divisions were escalating their competitive financial offers. "This is ridiculous," he complained. "We're raising the stakes in a bidding war against ourselves!"

This type of organizational dysfunction is not unusual. Have you observed it where you work? It occurs when people lose sight of the common good and seek to advance their own interests—even at the expense of colleagues. An individual who can break through this dysfunction and get contending parties to recognize the common good and work toward it together stands to gain substantial influence with both the antagonists and senior management. He or she gains respect as an unbiased defender of the common good.

To be successful in this endeavor, take a lesson from experienced decision makers: Develop a set of feasible alternatives, or solutions, one or more of which will satisfy the interests of the contending parties *and* the larger organization—in other words, a win-win-win solution. Too often, people latch onto a single solution that works for them and never look beyond it. In our Gemini Company example, each division saw a single solution: Convince the author to write a book to serve its own market. This created a self-destructive bidding war. However, a manager in the trade book division thought of an alternative that neither side had considered: Create a two-book deal—one trade book and one textbook. The author would complete one manuscript after the other. Since the two books would be based on a common body of information, this seemed practical and logical.

Each of the two divisions liked this alternative but only if it would be the first in line for the author's work. This created an impasse. Once again, the enterprising manager came through with a possible solution: Engage a professional writer to work with the author in developing the two books *simultaneously*. Again, this seemed feasible given the common body of information. Representatives of the text and trade book divisions liked the idea. Each division would attain its goal, and the corporation would add an eminent scholar to its stable of authors. The enterprising manager who dreamed up these alternatives and guided discussion about them helped people find common ground. In so doing, he gained stature in the eyes of everyone concerned, and his influence in the organization rose by equal measure.

Perhaps you, like the manager in this example, can help the people where you work find common ground. Here are some tips for succeeding:

➤ Prepare yourself by developing a solid understanding of your organization's key goals. Your solutions must be aligned with one or more of these goals.

➤ Discover the interests of the other parties—the things they *want* that will provide real benefits. Caution: Interests may be masked by the parties' stated "positions," which are not the same as their real interests. In our example, the textbook division's *position* might be this: "We found this climate-change expert, and we insist that that he sign a contract with us and not with you." The division's *interest*, however, is in obtaining a revenue-generating product. This is very different from its position.

➤ Develop the mental habit of creating *several alternative solutions* whenever you confront a problem. Don't become attached to any of these solutions until you've objectively analyzed each one.

➤ Work toward the solution from which the parties *and* the organization will obtain the greatest value.

FRAME THE ISSUE YOUR WAY

Another tactic for gaining influence is to encourage people to frame important issues your way—that is, to see them as you do. A *frame* is the mental window through which we view reality. It influences how we see, hear, and interpret the world around us. If, for example, you asked an economist to assess what's going on in the Detroit area, he or she would describe the problems of the area's automakers, and how those problems have spilled over to the region's supplier companies, causing cascading waves of unemployment, reduced tax revenues, and so forth. This economist's mind is wired to see the situation in terms of production, employment, wages, and revenues. That's his frame. A trained sociologist's assessment of the Detroit area would be different. The sociologist would focus on how lost jobs and wages are affecting family relationships, crime, and community stability. Psychologist Kelton

Rhoads uses the murder trial of O.J. Simpson as an example of how the right frame can influence a jury. Simpson's legal team, he reminds us, framed the case as one of an innocent black man versus a racist police department. That frame was adopted by the jury with the result that police evidence was seen by most jury members as unreliable, if not planted. And Simpson was found not guilty.

How are people framing the important issues facing your company or work group? Chances are that the frame people accept will define the boundaries of subsequent discussion and the ultimate resolutions of those issues. Thus, if you can get people to adopt your frame, you will have exerted substantial influence over eventual decisions and actions. Consider the following example:

As head of human resources, Pauline is being badgered by Ned, a department manager. Ned insists that he doesn't have enough people to handle his unit's workload. "We're already asking some people to come in on Saturdays," he complains, "yet we continue to fall behind." But Pauline's hands are tied. Top management insists that the head count be kept in check. Nevertheless, Pauline and her staff quietly begin studying Ned's problem.

Seeing that he is getting nowhere with Pauline, Ned goes to the COO, her boss, with the issue. Pauline soon finds herself in a meeting with the COO and the disgruntled manager. Ned proceeds to make his case for relaxing the hiring freeze and allowing him to hire two new people. When he finishes, the COO turns to Pauline and says, "So, what's your response? We don't have new positions in the budget, but we can't allow Ned's people to keep falling behind either."

Instead of questioning the points made by Ned, Pauline redirects the discussion entirely. "What we have here isn't a manpower problem; it's a work process problem." She goes on to explain how her staff's initial mapping of the department's work processes uncovered time-sapping handoffs and bottlenecks. Some activities appeared to add more cost than value. "Approaching Ned's situation as a traditional manpower problem isn't the answer," Pauline explains. "We in HR think it would be more productive to work with Ned on process improvements with the goal of making the work faster and less labor intensive. This will solve Ned's problem and comply with the company's hiring freeze."

In this case, Pauline attempts to shift the COO's and Ned's framing of the problem: from having too few people to having an inefficient work process. If she succeeds, she will have influenced an important decision—and scored points with both Ned and her boss.

Can you think of situations in which you might exert influence by framing the problem or the issue? In many cases, you will find framing opportunities by applying a lesson learned in the previous section: by thinking of and examining alternative solutions. Pauline's framing of Ned's problem as a work process issue, for example, originates in an alternative—one that Pauline found outside the box of Ned's conventional solution. In other cases, you need to embrace a different viewpoint. For example, if a group of employees insist that they should get a 5 percent wage hike this year because they received no increase last year, you might reframe the issue this way: "I appreciate your interest in a raise. But you're already receiving premium wages. We're currently paying you $3 per hour more than what our competitor is paying its people for the same work."

Change the way people frame the issue, and you will influence subsequent debate and decisions. Framing can also be used to influence people to adopt different, more productive behaviors. This is particularly important when leading change. Change requires that people abandon the status quo and do things differently: restructure their work, team up with other people, learn new skills, and so forth. Some people resist change because the status quo for them is profitable, comfortable, and seems safe. Others resist change when they see themselves as coming out as losers.

The leader who frames change as a set of distasteful and difficult chores will have little influence on people's behavior. With no appealing carrot to dangle before them, he will have nothing but the stick to motivate change. By framing change in positive terms—as necessary and beneficial—the leader will be much more successful in altering behavior and maintaining morale.

BUILD A NETWORK OF SUPPORT

Do you lack organizational power? Are you competing for influence against people who have it and know how to use it? Welcome to reality. Organizational life doesn't always provide a level playing field for competing ideas. People outside the inner sanctum of decision making often find themselves at a disadvantage. Their ideas are not recognized or solicited, and access to decision makers is often blocked. Not every company operates this way. Back in the days when founders Bill Hewlett and David Packard ran HP, employees understood that they could go directly to Bill's or Dave's office if they had something important to say. Likewise, Motorola had a policy of accommodating open dissent that made it possible for engineers, managers, and other employees to publicly argue with their bosses on matters of interest to the company's future. If an engineer's or a bench scientist's new product idea was turned down by an immediate superior, he or she could appeal to a higher-level decision maker.[3] That type of openness is commendable, but seldom seen.

One way to level the playing field of influence is to develop a network of support. It's easy for a lone employee who lacks power to be ignored or discounted; it is much harder to ignore someone who enjoys the support of many in the organization. The "strength in numbers" concept is widely understood and implemented by unions, coalitions, and alliances. A union steward has more influence over management than he would as an ordinary employee. A coalition of environmental groups has greater clout with a congressional representative than would any member group on its own. When a start-up pharmaceutical company allies with a larger company that has broad distribution, its potential market impact is greatly multiplied. You too can enhance your influence by building a supportive network.

Whether people recognize it or not, just about everyone in a workplace participates in a network. Your network includes the following people:

> Those with whom you collaborate and share information—for example, the informal group that meets for lunch occasionally to swap ideas for cutting through red tape

> Those on whom you depend when you're in a jam—for example, the woman in the warehouse you call when a replacement part must be rushed to a key customer

> Those who depend on you to make them look good—for example, the colleague who relies on you to create the electronic spreadsheet models she cannot figure out how to do

> Those with whom you're personally simpatico—for example, the guy in the finance department who was on your college rowing team

➤ Those with whom you share important workplace goals—for example, the four people on your product development team

You won't find your network on the organization chart. That chart indicates official reporting relationships. Your network is un-official, ad hoc, unmapped, and held together by mutual needs, common aspirations, and personal bonds. It operates in the spaces between the tidy chart boxes. Don't be surprised if your network includes peers and people above and below you in the pecking order of authority.

So, you already have a network. But how much does it contrib-ute to your influence? Logically, your network contributes to the extent that its individual members:

➤ Have influence of their own
➤ Are recognized as important contributors to key organizational goals
➤ Have expertise or knowledge valued by management
➤ Are reckoned to be trustworthy and reliable (two foundation attributes of influence)
➤ Are supportive of you and your ideas
➤ Enjoy access to decision makers

The more your network reflects these qualities, the greater its potential contribution to your personal influence. Obtaining stand-ing in a network with these qualities requires effort on your part. You cannot claim it as a matter of right but must earn your place by:

➤ Being trustworthy and reliable in your dealings with others
➤ Providing support and doing favors for network members when asked

➤ Returning the favors done for you

➤ Contributing ideas and leadership

➤ Working with others toward shared goals

A network like the one we've described has no natural cap on member numbers, nor is it limited to particular departments or operating units. As an instrument of your influence, it will ideally extend into every area of the organization where you'd like to have an impact, and from which you'd like to gather information and support. So keep your eyes open for potential new members of your network. When you find them, get to know these people on a personal level. Then find ways to help them be more successful in their work. Share your ideas and gain their support. If you do this deliberately over a period of months and years, you will build personal influence and an army of support.

EMPLOY PERSUASIVE COMMUNICATION

Persuasion is a process of communication through which one person alters the beliefs, attitudes, or actions of others. In organizations, it's difficult to find a person with substantial influence who lacks the ability to persuade.

Persuasive communication has less to do with verbal fluency than with (1) understanding people's needs and interests, and (2) using language and arguments that address them effectively.

. . . .

IT ALL GOES BACK TO ATHENS

The roots of persuasion as a discipline go back to fourth-century BCE Athens, where Aristotle developed and taught his

Rhetoric as an audience-centered approach to gaining the assent of listeners. Later published as three books, Aristotelian rhetoric was studied by aspiring politicians and leaders of the Greco-Roman world as well as public figures of the Renaissance, and it continues to be read today. Book II of *Rhetoric* is concerned with the art of persuasion, which Aristotle regarded as having three enabling elements for the orator: credibility, the emotions and psychology of the audience, and logical reasoning. Those three elements are as potent today as they were in the golden age of Greece.

. . . .

Understanding

People with no sales experience often think of successful salespeople as motormouths—manipulative "slick talkers" who can sell refrigerators to Eskimos. This perception is inaccurate. The truth is that effective salespeople spend less time talking about what they have to sell than trying to understand how they can help customers satisfy their needs, achieve their goals, or overcome problems and frustrations. And when they actually get around to describing their products or services, they put less emphasis on the *features* of what they're selling than on the *benefits* that customers will experience. This approach to other people begins with listening.

Good communicators know that they learn nothing while they're talking. Consequently, their initial conversations with people are used to probe, to clarify, and to signal that they are giving people their full attention. For example:

Probing

➤ "What is the biggest problem you're having?"
➤ "Have you thought about simplifying that process?"

- ➤ "What do you need to get this job done by the end of the month?"

Clarifying

- ➤ "I don't understand. Could you run that by me again?"
- ➤ "You said that your team doesn't have enough resources. What resources are you talking about?"
- ➤ "I'm trying to understand if this problem is our fault or someone else's. What do you think?"

Signaling

- ➤ "If I understand you, the end-of-month deadline isn't realistic."
- ➤ "So, you think that we could completely eliminate that step without reducing quality, right?"
- ➤ "I'm with you so far. Tell me more."

Skilled communicators let other people talk. They know that this is the best way to get those people to reveal their interests, concerns, goals, and aspirations. Understanding these opens the door to persuasion and influence. Try to apply the three listening tactics just described—probing, clarifying, and signaling—the next time you engage in a conversation with your boss or coworkers. See what you can learn.

· ·

A PRACTICAL TEST

How well do you understand the people with whom you work? Try to answer the following questions:

1. What work problems keep your boss awake at night?

_____

_____

2. Consider one of your key subordinates. What is that person's career aspiration?

_____

_____

3. Identify a person outside your team or department with whom you interact regularly. What would make that person's job easier or make him or her more successful?

_____

_____

By understanding the interests and concerns of the people you aim to persuade, you'll be in a better position to bring them around to your view.

. . . .

Another part of understanding is the identification of key decision makers. In cases in which your intention is to influence a decision, you'll want to focus your persuasion on the people who will determine the outcome. Understanding the decision-making process is equally important. For example, if your intention is to persuade management to develop a new product, you need to be able to answer the following questions:

➤ Who will make the _final_ decision?
➤ To whom do the decision makers turn for advice on new product development?

➤ What is the process for making decisions about new products? Is there a formal process, such as a stage-gate system? Is the decision in the hands of a single executive or of a committee?

If you fail to answer these questions, your efforts to persuade may be directed toward the wrong people.

Once you understand how decisions are made, your task is to identify the key players and thought leaders. *Thought leaders* are the people whom others listen to when important matters are on the table. These individuals may have organizational power. They may be managers or executives. They may have technical expertise. Or they may simply possess the good business sense that commands respect from others. Even when these individuals do not make decisions, thought leaders often influence the people who do.

Key decision makers and thought leaders are the people on whom you should focus your persuasive communication. Just be careful, though; the person you assume to be the decision maker may be highly influenced by one or more people you wouldn't expect to have that power.

· ·

DRAW AN INFLUENCE MAP

One way to systematically understand who influences whom is to sketch out an influence map—a graphic representation of the patterns and strength of influence. The map shown in this sidebar indicates who is influencing whom—and how much—in a six-person department. One outsider, Val, is included. The arrows indicate the direction of influence, and the thickness of each arrow gives a rough idea of the strength of that influence, with the thickest arrows representing the strongest influence. Note that influence between individuals is usually a two-way street. For instance, Stan, the boss, strongly influences Jane and Fran, his subordinates; Fran and Jane influence Stan, but to a lesser degree. The broken line between Val and Stan indicates Val's indirect influence (through Jane) on Stan.

As you can imagine, there is no way to map influences with precision. There's nothing empirically measurable here. But the mere exercise of mapping is useful in forcing us to think about who is influencing whom. What are the directions and strengths of influence in your immediate workplace? Just for fun, try mapping them.

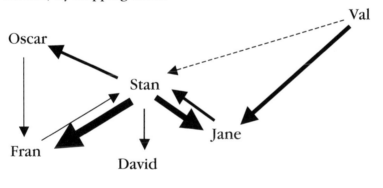

Persuasive Language

The language you use, and how you use language to frame your presentation, also affects your persuasiveness. In this section, we consider four aspects of language use:

1. Making a credible case

2. Speaking to both the head and the heart

3. Describing the features and benefits of your ideas

4. Engaging in positive, unqualified communication

Making a Credible Case

Successful persuasive communication requires a credible case based on logic and supported by evidence. Most people have a hard time saying no to logical arguments and evidence. Conversely, it's easy to dismiss a would-be persuader who hasn't done his homework—who hasn't developed a solid, fact-based case. This is especially true when a proposal requires people to change what they are doing or take a calculated risk.

Speaking to Both the Head and the Heart

A solid case can get you close to the finish line but you'll often need one more thing to carry you over—language that addresses the heart (emotions). Logical argument is head language, and it is most appropriate when a decision hinges on quantifiable information, and when the people involved are analytical and data oriented: accountants, engineers, strategic planners, stock analysts, and so forth. Head language appeals to the logical mind and its need for reliable evidence. A person negotiating the purchase of an established business, for example, will use that business's trail of revenues and operating expenses to explain why she is willing to pay only so much for the enterprise. "Here are data I've obtained on three recent sales of similar businesses in this area. In each case, the buyer paid no more than two times operating earnings, which is what I'm prepared to offer you today." In some cases, however, persuasion is more effective when it speaks to the heart.

> "Look, I simply cannot pay you more than $450,000 for your business. That's all it's worth and it's the best I can do. So, accept my offer and put this business and all its problems and chores behind you. Imagine how it will feel to wake up with $450,000 in your bank account and not a care in the world."

Great public speakers understand the power of an emotional appeal. Consider Winston Churchill's famous speech in the early days of World War II, when his island nation stood alone against the more powerful forces of Nazi Germany. Churchill did not cite statistics to his listeners. Instead, he spoke to their hearts, underscoring the courage they would need to carry on during the months ahead.

Even though large tracts of Europe and many old and famous states have fallen or may fall into the grip of the Gestapo and all the odious apparatus of Nazi rule, we shall not flag or fail.

We shall go on to the end, we shall fight in France, we shall fight on the seas and oceans, we shall fight with growing confidence and growing strength in the air, we shall defend our island, whatever the cost may be. We shall fight on the beaches, we shall fight on the landing grounds, we shall fight in the fields and in the streets, we shall fight in the hills; we shall never surrender. . . .[4]

In some cases, a successful appeal to the heart will outweigh weaknesses in the logical case.

Describing the Features and Benefits of Your Ideas

Language that plays up benefits also speaks to the heart. Pushing the "features" of one's case, in contrast, speaks to the head. Every salesperson knows the difference between features and benefits. When someone says, "This computer has a 2.33-megahertz processor and 3 gigabytes of DDR3 Tri-Channel SDRAM at 1066 megahertz," that person is describing features. Features are necessary in that they set the groundwork. You should communicate them, especially if your audience is technically oriented, or if the discussion calls for a full airing of the details. But many people are persuaded by benefits, not features. Here are some examples of persuasive speech that emphasizes benefits to listeners:

> "Because this is such a *fast* computer, you won't be sitting there waiting and waiting. And we all hate waiting. . . ."

> "If we adopt the new work process I've described, we will improve employee productivity by 20 percent. And that will save our department $180,000 every year. That's money we could share between our owners and employees."

> "If you are willing to accept my offer, I can have a check on your desk within twenty-four hours."

Engaging in Positive, Unqualified Communication

Some people cannot make an unqualified statement. "I think that_____" is their preferred opener to every statement:

"I think that this offer will benefit both of our companies."

"I think that we should change our process."

"I think that what we meant in that report was we might be able to save some time and money."

If you're trying to persuade someone to adopt your view, saying "I think that" is like saying "I'm not sure, but_____." These qualifications tell listeners that you lack confidence in your view, or that you're offering nothing but a personal opinion. And opinions aren't worth much. Instead, be affirmative:

"Our offer *will* benefit both companies."

"We *must* change our process."

"This *will* save us time and money."

Note how much stronger these statements are compared to the previous ones.

If you have built a credible case, you can make affirmative statements with confidence, and that confidence will inspire the same in your listeners.

◆　◆　◆　◆　◆

We've now offered six tactics you can use to gain influence at work. Some are bound to be more productive for you and seem more comfortable and natural than others. For best results, combine as many tactics as the situation allows.

The next chapter identifies the people in your work life whom you must influence. You're sure to find opportunities to employ your new tactics on them.

CHAPTER REVIEW

To review what you have learned, take the following open-book review quiz.

1. How does doing a favor for a workplace colleague or for your boss increase your influence over that person? What principle does the favor evoke?

_____

_____

_____

_____

2. How does being the "go-to person" with respect to expertise, information, or resources contribute to influence?

_____

_____

_____

_____

3. Helping others to find common ground is one tactic of influence. Describe a situation in your experience where this tactic was employed.

_____

_____

_____

_____

4. What is a mental frame?

_____

_____

_____

_____

5. Your workplace support network is strengthened when its members have particular characteristics. Can you name two?

_____

_____

_____

_____

6. What is the first task in persuading people?

_____

_____

_____

_____

NOTES

1. Allan R. Cohen and David L. Bradford, _Influence Without Authority_ (New York: John Wiley & Sons, 1991.), 29.

2. Thomas J. Peters and Robert H. Waterman, _In Search of Excellence_ (New York: Harper Collins, 1982), 32.

3. Richard Luecke, _Scuttle Your Ships Before Advancing_ (New York: Oxford University Press, 1993), 166.

4. From Winston Churchill's speech to the House of Commons of the British Parliament on the June 4, 1940.

CHAPTER 4

APPLYING INFLUENCE DOWN AND SIDEWAYS

T he previous two chapters described the foundation attributes of influential people and practical tactics you can apply in building influence where you work. By developing those personal attributes and engaging those tactics, you can—over time— have greater influence over the thinking and behavior of others. The next logical step is to apply your influence in productive ways to three groups of people with whom you routinely interact at work: your subordinates, your peers, and your boss (see Figure 4-1). The first two groups are discussed in this chapter; how to influence the boss is so special that we treat it separately in Chapter 5. Customers are another important constituency, and much of what is covered here can be applied to them.

INFLUENCING YOUR SUBORDINATES

The working world has changed a lot over the past twenty years. In the old days, managers were more direct in dealing with subordi-

FIGURE 4-1. INFLUENCING IN MANY DIRECTIONS.

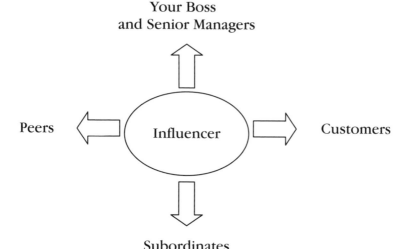

nates: Managers would tell; subordinates would do. In other words, managers relied more on formal power or authority and less on influence to get the results they wanted.

The workplace in those days was more sharply stratified by rank, with scores of worker bees at the bottom, a stack of lower and middle managers above them, and the Big Bosses at the tip-top. Communication followed a *command-and-control* model in which information about customers and operations flowed upward through the chain of command. Decisions were made in the executive suite, and orders were then sent downward through the same chain of command: "Do this; then do that."

Many companies have abandoned command-and-control management in favor of *employee empowerment*, a management model that gives subordinates greater discretion in how they accomplish their objectives. Managers tell their subordinates what needs to be accomplished but give them greater discretion in *how* the work should be done. Empowered employees are also given greater authority over company resources. For example, an employee who deals directly with customers may be authorized to give rebates, discounts, refunds, or other services in order to resolve problems or correct errors on the spot. Research indicates that empowerment contributes to greater initiative, motivation, and workplace satisfaction among employees. In addition, it has been shown that empowerment makes organizations faster in responding to customer needs and market conditions, reduces the number of middle managers needed, and puts decision makers in closer contact with the front lines of the business.

Employee empowerment has also greatly altered the manager-subordinate relationship. Power in the workplace isn't what it used to be. Subordinates expect to participate in work planning. The old lever of formal power has lost much of its effectiveness. Younger employees—so-called Gen X and Gen Y—are notoriously unmoved by command-and-control management. Power can be used in a pinch, but managers who resort to it often find themselves surrounded by a bunch of surly and unmotivated people who exert the least effort possible. To succeed in today's environment, managers have to put away the lever of command and apply influence.

Recollect our definition of influence: Like power, it is something we use *to get what we want* from others. For a manager, "what we want" is the achievement of goals for which he or she is held accountable. The manager who cannot influence subordinates to achieve those goals has recourse to only one lever in getting results: the power to command. But that lever, as we've explained, isn't very effective in today's workplace. Managers and supervisors must determine when and when not to use it.

Several members of Susan's busy insurance office usually arrive a few minutes late, then spend fifteen minutes getting coffee, chatting, booting up their computers, and checking e-mails. As branch manager, Susan *could* stand at the door demonstrably checking her watch and write up disciplinary notices for chronic latecomers. This would probably force compliance, but not inspire cooperation or team spirit. Instead, Susan speaks to the team: "I know some of us have long drives to get here, but the doors open at 9:00 and it's not fair to our customers to make them queue up for just a few desks. And it's not fair to Mack and Jenny to be swamped while the rest of us drink our coffee." Then every day Susan makes sure she herself is at her desk working at 9:00 sharp and greets each employee pleasantly as he or she arrives.

In this example, Susan has opted to influence her subordinates by means of persuasive language and by her personal example. So how can you influence subordinates? For the answer, let's revisit the foundation attributes and the tactics of influence, as described earlier (see Figure 4-2). These are the levers managers and supervisors can pull to get the results they want.

Trust

In influencing subordinates, your trustworthiness is essential. The people who work for you must trust in your word. They must also trust that you will recognize and respect their interests. When you tell people that something is important, and prevail upon them to make an extra effort, there should be no doubts about your verac-

FIGURE 4-2. FOUNDATION ATTRIBUTES AND TACTICS OF INFLUENCE.

Foundation Attributes	Tactics
Trustworthiness	Create reciprocal credits.
Reliability	Be a source of expertise, information, and resources.
Assertiveness	Help people find common ground.
	Frame issues your way.
	Build a network of support.
	Employ persuasive communication.

ity. They should trust that it's important to you *and to them*. Otherwise subordinates will mutter, "She's always advancing herself on our backs." Being a team player—someone who shares in the rigors of team-based work—is a good way to build trust and to assure people that you are working toward mutual interests.

Few circumstances illustrate the importance of trust better than the relationships that develop between small-unit military leaders and their people. Low- and midlevel officers (lieutenants and captains) who work closely with subordinates, sharing their hardships and soliciting their ideas, generate a level of trust that makes "pulling rank" seldom necessary. Soldiers accept the directives of these officers out of a sense that they would never ask them to do something they wouldn't do themselves. If you're a manager, you can accomplish the same by being visibly involved in the work. Directing subordinates from a cozy office simply won't do. And if you ask them to put in extra effort on the weekend, don't regale them Monday morning with tales about your adventures at the yacht club!

Managers also generate influence-enhancing trust when they share information that affects their subordinates. The practice of "open book management" (OBM) is one example of information sharing that improves performance. OBM provides employees with all relevant financial and performance information about their company or unit. Evidence shows that employees feel more involved with their jobs and make better day-to-day decisions if they are regularly updated on company revenues, cash flow, expenses, and profitability. Information sharing of this type also enhances trust. Let's face it, people who are kept in the dark are justifiably suspicious and distrustful. If management says, "Today we're announcing a company-wide campaign to reduce expenses, and we expect everyone to pitch in," employees are as likely to dig in their heels as to cooperate. Conversely, if all employees can see that profitability is being squeezed by flagging revenues and increasing costs, the necessity of expense reduction will be apparent, and those same employees will find numerous ways to cut costs. As a manager, you can get the benefits of OBM by sharing the three or four critical performance measures that are *under the control* of your unit and its people.

One company we know has been very effective using this approach. The company attacks its important problems and opportunities through cross-functional teams of five to seven employees. Each team has what it calls "critical performance indicators" (CPIs), and each team focuses on a fairly narrow, measurable goal deemed important to the company. One team, for example, is working to enhance the experience of people who use the company's website. That team's CPIs include page feed times, the number of minutes that people stay on the website, and the number of people who return to the website each week. Team CPIs are compiled and posted via e-mail every afternoon. Everyone knows how things are going, what progress is being made, and what problems are surfacing. That kind of openness generates trust between employees and their managers.

As a manager, you have plenty of nonconfidential information that can be shared with subordinates. Here are just a few examples:

> Monthly unit/dollar sales.

> Updates on company-wide initiatives, such as installing an enterprise software system.

> Variances from budgeted sales or expenses; these give employees at-a-glance indications of what's going well and poorly, and where interventions should be made.

Information sharing on matters such as these opens the door to productive dialogue and idea exchanges, both of which engender trust between subordinates and their managers—the kind of trust that makes influence possible.

Persuasion

Beyond developing trust, managers must also learn the fine art of persuasion. Persuasion, as we've defined it, is communication that alters the beliefs, attitudes, or actions of others. As noted in Chapter 3, persuasive communication has less to do with being a slick talker than with understanding people's needs and interests, and then applying language and logical arguments that address them in positive ways. Now, let's consider how you can use persuasive communication to influence the people who report to you.

Let's begin with needs and interests. Do you understand the needs and interests of your subordinates? At one level, human needs in the workplace are pretty universal. Back in the 1950s,

Abraham Maslow, a pioneer in the field of industrial psychology, theorized a hierarchy of human needs, as shown in Figure 4-3. Maslow believed that lower-level needs had to be satisfied before people would concern themselves with higher-level needs. For example, a person who hasn't satisfied his need for safety (i.e., job security and a reliable income) is unlikely to be concerned with his need for esteem (self-respect, confidence, etc.). Likewise, a person who has satisfied certain needs will stop fretting about those and begin to reach higher on the needs ladder. Thus, the subordinate whose physiological, safety, and affiliation needs have been met will start to address his need for esteem.

In a nutshell, Maslow's theory is that people's needs are never fully satisfied until they reach the top of the ladder: *self-actualization*. Self-actualization is the feeling people have when they are in control of their lives, and when they sense that they are exploiting their full potential.

Take a moment to think about the people who report directly

FIGURE 4-3. MASLOW'S HIERARCHY OF HUMAN NEEDS.

Self-Actualization	In control of one's life; exploiting one's potential
Esteem	Self-worth, self-respect, recognition
Affiliation	Friendship, being part of the group
Safety	Economic security, safe conditions
Physiological	Food, water, shelter, income

to you. How high has each climbed on the hierarchy of needs? If you can figure that out, you'll have an idea of each subordinate's next unsatisfied need. That unsatisfied need is what the person is concerned about—what makes him or her feel anxious, uncomfortable, or unmotivated. For example:

> Helen, a newly hired clerical worker, is struggling toward the "affiliation" level. After six months on the job, she still feels like an outsider and would like to fit in and be an accepted member of the work group.
>
> Greg's prowess as a salesperson is widely praised within the company. He is firmly perched on the "esteem" level but is feeling dissatisfied with his lack of control over his life at work. After ten years of selling the same products to the same customers, he's bored and feeling unfulfilled. He'd like to develop other skills and take on a larger role in the company.

In these examples, Helen and Greg have identifiable unmet needs. Their boss could use an understanding of those needs to craft persuasive communications and to motivate these individuals. If you were Greg's boss, for instance, and wanted a customer research project done, you might target Greg for the assignment and tantalize him with the prospect of doing something that is new to him and that he could control, and that represents an expanded role for him within the company. By channeling your persuasive communication through what *Greg* wants, you would increase your influence with him and stand a better chance of getting what *you* want. He would very likely take on your project without objection. And because Greg would view you as someone who recognizes his needs, your influence with him would extend into the future: "Yes, my boss understands and addresses my interests at work. I can trust her."

The Velvet-Gloved Fist

We stated earlier that you should avoid exercising your organizational power whenever other tools of influence are available. In an age of employee empowerment, you should reach for the power lever only when you absolutely must. However, your power can be used in the background to persuade and influence the behavior of others.

President Theodore Roosevelt popularized the adage, "Speak softly and carry a big stick." The U.S. Marine Corps advertises itself as "No greater friend, no worse enemy." In each case, someone with real power has made this clear: "There are large benefits to playing ball with me; the costs of not playing ball are even greater." We call this the velvet-gloved fist tactic of persuasion and influence.

As a manager you have, within limits, the power to hire and fire, to promote or demote, to determine who receives increased compensation and who doesn't, to decide who receives the plum assignment and who will work the graveyard shift, and so forth. A deft manager knows how to subtly exercise those powers in ways that let people get the message and respond. For example:

Although nothing was said by the department manager, people notice that Bill and Betty—enthusiastic supporters of their boss's new pet project—were chosen to attend this year's trade show in Hawaii. In January, no less. Meanwhile, Bob and Beatrice, who haven't gotten on board the project, have been

asked to represent the company at an ice-fishing festival in
northern Minnesota that same month.

Like laboratory mice, people sense and respond to signals of
reward and punishment, often without noticing. If you are subtle
but consistent in how you extend and withhold rewards, you can
make the velvet-gloved fist tactic work for you.

INFLUENCING YOUR PEERS

Most of us must collaborate with others. We are members of work
teams, each applying our special know-how to some aspects of the
total job. By collaborating, we get things done. Or we are members
of ad hoc task forces that come together to jointly solve a particular
problem, and then return to our regular assignments. Even outside
salespeople who seldom set foot in the office find that they must
interact and collaborate via phone or e-mail with support personnel if they hope to generate and fill customer orders. The same is
true of the estimated 25 percent of the U.S. workforce that does
some or all of its work from home or satellite locations.

Substantial collaborative work is transacted between *peers*—
people of roughly equal organizational standing. By definition, a
person has no authority to demand or command compliance from
a peer. For example, you cannot order your team member Jennifer,
who doesn't work for you, to do anything. If she's slacking on the
job and holding back team progress, you cannot order her to shape
up. You have only two choices: (1) ask your mutual boss—who has
the formal authority to order compliance—to deal with Jennifer, or
(2) find a way to *influence* her to do better work.

Your inability to affect your peers' performance through organizational power makes influence extremely important. It may be the only lever you have for getting what you want. In addition to the tactics you've already studied, the following sections explain three tactics you can use to influence your peers:

1. Create reciprocal credits.
2. Build a network of support.
3. Implement peer influence.

Creating Reciprocal Credits

We described the universally accepted principle of reciprocity in Chapter 3. Every time you do something for someone, you create an IOU that must someday and in some manner be repaid. Every IOU provides you with a measure of influence with that person. Consider this example:

Roland and Sarah are midlevel managers working for a health products firm. Roland manages production scheduling and Sarah is in charge of new-product introductions for the marketing unit. Each was assigned last year to a task force whose job is to plan the company's move of personnel, furnishings, and equipment to a new office building the following spring. The team anticipated biweekly meetings over a ten-month period to develop that plan.

Roland was chosen by his teammates to act as leader, a position that carries with it no formal power to command. Recognizing his situation, Roland works hard to develop consensus on a moving plan. Sarah has been an impediment to that consensus.

Sarah is independent minded and has strong views about the move that others will not support. This has made the hoped-for consensus unlikely. Believing that her collaboration is essential, Roland has begun a campaign to influence her views.

Outside the planning team structure, the two managers occasionally interact on other business. Sarah, for example, was faced with introducing five new over-the-counter drugs later in the year, which required coordination with Roland. And she had a serious problem.

"Roland, I'm in a bind. Perhaps you can help me."

"What's the problem, Sarah?"

"Well, the R&D people have fallen a month behind schedule in formulating our five new OTC products—the ones whose production schedules we discussed last month. As it stands now, I can't get you those formulas until November 15."

"Yes, that is a problem," said Roland. "I scheduled your production and shipping based on your assurance that we'd have those formulas in mid-October. This delay will set back production by two months at least."

"I was afraid of that," she responded glumly. "And that would be a disaster. We've already purchased ad media for the planned launch and the salespeople are holding millions of dollars in customer orders with firm delivery dates in late November."

Sarah was in a very bad spot. The success of her product launches would be jinxed if Roland couldn't promise the original production and shipping schedule. Roland recognized her distress, but he couldn't hold to the original schedule if she couldn't provide the new drug formulas as promised. Ingredients had to be ordered and delivered by suppliers—and they had lead-time needs of their own.

This was Sarah's problem, not Roland's. Nevertheless, he wanted to help. So, over the next few days he did some investigating, made calls to a number of suppliers, and persuaded another manager to accept a noncritical delay in the production of his products. By the end of the week he was able to give Sarah some good news.

"I want you to know that I can give you the original production and shipping date just as long as your R&D schedule doesn't slip again," Roland said.

"That's great!" she replied. "I really appreciate it, Roland."

We frequently observe situations similar to this example in business operations. Someone finds herself in a bind, calls a peer in another department, and asks for help. And when help is rendered, a reciprocal obligation is created. That obligation creates an opportunity to exert influence. You can bet that Roland will use that opportunity to gain Sarah's acceptance of their team's consensus plan. Roland will probably not refer directly to the "debt"; simply having gone the extra mile for Sarah may be enough to soften her resistance. Sure, she may still object to aspects of the plan, but the fact that she owes Roland a favor may be sufficient to neutralize her objection and bring her on board.

This illustrative case underscores a tactic that you can use to good effect in influencing your peers: Learn as much as you can about your peers, then, like Roland, be alert for opportunities to help them be more successful in their work. This might involve:

> ➤ Sharing resources you control that they need

> ➤ Providing expert advice

> ➤ Acting as an intermediary or go-between with some other source of resources

> ➤ Rearranging your schedule (as Roland did) to accommodate theirs

> ➤ Satisfying the human need to feel accepted and appreciated

In many cases, actions like these will cost you little or nothing, yet they can increase your influence. What can you do for your peers that would create in them an influence-engendering sense of obligation to you?

. . . .

WHO DEPENDS ON YOU?

As long as we're on the subject of reciprocity, we should mention a related concept: dependency. Every one of us is dependent on one or more people for success in the workplace. We depend on our bosses for the resources we need to do our jobs. We depend on our subordinates to do their jobs on time and to do them right—our own performance reviews would take a beating if they didn't! We also depend on our peers for things we value: information ("What can you tell me about this new CFO?") and support ("Roland's flexibility in production scheduling has saved my bacon once again!"). When processes are linear, we depend on other units to hand off the work to us on schedule. Like reciprocity, you can often use a peer's dependence on you to exert influence on him or her.

. . . .

The Favor Effect

The principle of reciprocity has an odd twist, which we refer to as the *favor effect*. Its source is a maxim cited by Benjamin Franklin: "He that has once done you a kindness will be more ready to do you another than he whom yourself have obliged." In other words, if you ask someone for a favor, and he or she complies, that person will be disposed to do you another favor. As evidence, Franklin relates in his autobiography the story of a fellow legislator in the Pennsylvania House, a political opponent who had been personally hostile to Franklin. Franklin decided that he would win the man's friendship, not by being servile, but by—of all things—asking a special favor:

> Having heard that he had in his library a certain very scarce
> and curious book, I wrote a note to him expressing my
> desire of perusing that book and requesting he would do
> me the favour of lending it to me for a few days.[1]

The man immediately sent Franklin the book, which Franklin returned shortly thereafter with a note expressing his gratitude for the favor. Their relationship then changed dramatically:

> When we next met in the House he spoke to me (which he
> had never done before), and with great civility; and he ever
> afterward manifested a readiness to serve me on all occa-
> sions, so that we became great friends.[2]

Modern social psychologists have confirmed Franklin's maxim through experiments, demonstrating that the giver of the favor ends up being more positively disposed to the asker than he was *before* the favor was requested. However, owing to the limited scope of these experiments, readers should be judicious in trying to apply this approach. Franklin's new friend probably took great pride in his personal library, and Franklin's request to borrow one of its rare holdings would naturally have been highly flattering. In effect, Franklin tipped his hat to the man's literary prowess and to the value of his collection. Thus, consider asking a favor from a person who is *proud* of having a particular resource or capability. For example, if you need help in negotiating with a difficult yet important client, you might ask for help from a person who prides herself on her negotiating skill. By asking the favor, you, in effect, recognize that person's special talent, as if saying "I came to you for help because you're such a good negotiator." People appreciate that kind of recognition and ego boost, especially when they feel that their special talent is not recognized or is undervalued. Your recognition of a person's special talent will create a bond between the two of you, opening a channel of influence.

Building a Network of Support

Back in Chapter 3 we cited building a network of support as a tactic for creating the bargaining power you lack as an individual employee. A network gives you "strength in numbers." Being part of a support network also gives you an opportunity to exert influence over your peers, many of whom may be part of that same network.

While membership in a network is valuable in itself, *active* membership will maximize your potential for influence. By active membership we mean being a positive contributor. A positive contributor does more than enjoy the benefits of membership. He or she is quick to offer help (information, resources, advice) to others and takes the lead when others hold back. These practices generate

IOUs on your behalf and make you more visible within the organization.

Here are three practical steps you can take to expand your network and influence:

1. Volunteer for task forces and special projects. Membership in these will give you opportunities to work with people in other parts of the organization, often at different levels. Also, by participating in the decisions and recommendations made by these entities, you will be influencing your organization's direction.

2. Introduce yourself to peers in other departments. Meet with them informally to learn of their concerns and responsibilities, and how your departments can work together more effectively. Make it a point to eat lunch with a different peer each week.

3. Form a *community of interest* around a topic considered important within the broader organization—for example, energy efficiency, telecommunications/IT improvements, innovation, quality. Communities of interest meet periodically to share ideas, information, and best-practice solutions for common concerns.

These action steps are not risky, difficult, or time-consuming, yet they will make you and your ideas more visible and influential among your peer group.

The same principle of reciprocity applies to online social-networking sites, such as LinkedIn. By adding contacts to your network, you make a tacit agreement to help them when you can, and expect them to reciprocate.

Implementing Peer Influence

We cannot leave this section without reference to *peer influence*, or peer pressure, which is the influence that group values and behaviors exert on individuals. You're surely familiar with this form of influence. We experienced it ourselves recently when a regular member of our morning fitness group dropped out with the intention of adopting a "do it yourself" approach. "I know all the exercise routines," he told us later, "so I figured I'd do them at home on my own and save the monthly fee." After a month, our friend gave up on his self-directed fitness routine and returned to the group. "It just wasn't the same," he said. "Instead of going for a full minute of push-ups, I'd put in thirty to forty seconds, then quit. Instead of our usual ten-minute run-sprint-run-sprint routine, I'd jog for ten minutes. I just didn't have the willpower to do the sprints." Our friend also admitted to skipping many workout days.

Why had our friend's plan failed? In his own words, it was the absence of peer pressure: "Without the trainer and you guys there to push me on, it was easy to slack off."

Examples of peer influence in the workplace are not hard to find. When people are working late to meet a group deadline, few people will have the nerve to say, "It's five o'clock. I'm going home." When a work group adopts high standards as a value, woe to whoever does shoddy work. Even when it lacks authority to punish individual malefactors, the group has the power to withhold the respect and acceptance that most people crave.

How can you put the power of peer influence to work? One way is through example. Let's say that you're the informal leader of a cross-functional team. You have no power over other team members. They're your peers, not your subordinates. But a big deadline looms and you'd like to influence them to work late every night for a week or two in order to finish the job on time. If you ask them politely to pitch in, and then very *visibly* continue working past five o'clock, you may get one or two of your peers to join in. And when the others see you working late *together*, peer pressure will encourage them to join in. People naturally feel uncomfortable when they are out of line with the larger group.

Personal example is a powerful influencer. A team of researchers confirmed this in an experiment they conducted in a busy New York City subway station. There they counted the number of people who tossed money into a street musician's hat. They then altered the conditions. Whenever someone was approaching, an accomplice of the researchers would stride by and tip the musician. This influenced others to do the same. In fact, a person who witnessed someone tip the musician was *eight times* more likely to drop money into the hat![3] That's peer influence at work.

If you want to influence peers or others through example, whatever you're doing must be visible, as in the case of the musician tipper. Let's suppose you'd like your workmates to be more energy conscious. The following strategies could be implemented to create wider visibility:

➤ **Use company media.** You might write an article for the company newsletter that features the energy-saving strategies used by people in several different departments.

➤ **Cast the desired behavior in a favorable light.** You might ask the company to create a monthly award program through which it honors individuals or departments that have done the most to reduce energy use.

◆ ◆ ◆ ◆ ◆

You can accomplish a great deal by applying appropriate tactics of influence to your subordinates and peers. But the greatest payoff may come when you apply them to the most important individual in your workplace life: your boss. You'll read all about how to do this in Chapter 5.

CHAPTER REVIEW

To review what you have learned, take the following open-book review quiz.

1. Explain how a manager or supervisor can establish trust between him or her and his or her subordinates.

_____

_____

_____

_____

2. What is the highest-level need in Maslow's hierarchy of human needs?

_____

_____

_____

_____

3. Identify two tactics for increasing one's influence over peers in the workplace.

_____

_____

_____

_____

NOTES

1. *The Autobiography of Benjamin Franklin*, online edition, page 48, accessed at http://www.ushistory.org/franklin/autobiography/page48.htm.
2. Ibid, 48.
3. Vladas Griskevicious, Robert B. Cialdini, and Noah J. Goldstein, "Applying (and Resisting) Peer Influence," *MIT Sloan Management Review* 49, no. 2 (Winter 2008): 87.

CHAPTER 5

INFLUENCING YOUR BOSS

S ubordinates and peers are important people in your work life. But your boss is special because he or she is both an evaluator of your performance and the main source of the resources and rewards you seek. Your boss may also be the key to your career advancement.

Being able to influence your boss is critically important to your success as an employee. The extent to which you can influence that person will go a long way to determining:

➤ The level of resources you'll have available
➤ The opportunities you'll have for career growth
➤ The degree of autonomy you'll be given
➤ Your financial rewards
➤ Mutual success

If your boss trusts and has confidence in you, he or she will welcome your participation in planning and decision making, which will give you a major level of control over your life at work. Having no influence, in contrast, will reduce you to being an order taker—a person who simply does what he or she is told.

INFLUENTIAL PEOPLE

History provides examples of subordinates who exerted substantial influence over their bosses. Few fit the bill better than France's Armand-Jean du Plessis de Richelieu (1585–1642). Richelieu, a provincial cleric when he entered public life, proved himself a reliable and effective second to a series of superiors, and he eventually became a cardinal of the church and the power behind the throne of France. His first political job came in 1614 when he was chosen as assistant to Concino Concini, the kingdom's most powerful minister. Concini was so pleased with his subordinate's performance that he elevated him to the position of Secretary of State, with responsibility for foreign affairs. Richelieu did well in this post. He also managed to survive the assassinations and intrigues of the court, and through talent and his own machinations he rose to the post of First Chief Minister to King Louis XIII. As First Chief Minister, there was hardly a matter of state that Richelieu did not touch: finances, war, diplomacy, appointments, and public works. His spy network within France and in the capitals of Europe made him a key source of information. That, his reliability, and his political and diplomatic acumen made him indispensable to the king, who looked to him for advice and the execution of policy.

Not surprisingly, many within the court were jealous of Richelieu's influence over the king and national policy, to the point that Louis's mother demanded that he dismiss Richelieu. After weighing the relative values of his mother and of his First Chief Minister,

Louis opted to keep Richelieu and send his mother into exile. He could manage without her, but not without Richelieu.

Similar examples of upward influence can be found in the world of business. Bill Gates of Microsoft relied heavily on Paul Allen until the latter's illness, then recruited another influential second in command in Steve Ballmer. Many credit Warren Buffett as the most acute mind in finance, yet Buffett would be the first to credit his longtime associate Charlie Munger for much of his and Berkshire Hathaway's success over the years.

Influence with one's boss is based on a relationship in which the boss:

➤ Trusts you

➤ Likes you

➤ Perceives you as similar in some ways to him or her

➤ Believes you have good and accurate information to share

➤ Depends on you to complement his or her strengths

➤ Is persuaded by your reasoning

➤ Considers you reliable and competent

➤ Recognizes an obligation to you for valued favors

➤ Believes you are working hard on the things that matter most to him or her

. . . .

ONE STUDY'S FINDINGS

A study conducted by scholars at the University of Illinois concluded that upward influence was related to a boss's perceptions of a subordinate's interpersonal skills, a liking for the subordinate, and perceptions of similarity between the boss and the subordinate. The subordinate's use of reasoning, assertiveness, and favor rendering (the "reciprocity" concept discussed earlier) was positively related to the boss's perceptions, whereas bargaining and self-promotion by the subordinate affected those perceptions negatively.[1]

. . . .

You too can enjoy influence with your boss if you follow the advice in the following sections.

MAKE SURE YOUR BOSS KNOWS HE OR SHE CAN TRUST YOU

Trust is important in any relationship, especially if you want to exercise influence. But trust is absolutely critical in your relationship with your boss. Your boss looks to you to accomplish your departmental objectives, thereby making him or her look good. More than that, your boss needs to know that you will always tell the *whole* truth, the good news and the bad. There must be no unpleasant surprises, especially public ones! Your boss will not trust you if you violate the chain of command and go around him or her to confer with his or her superior without first clearing it. If you seem to be vying for your boss's job, don't expect to be rewarded with trust!

FOCUS ON WHAT'S IMPORTANT TO YOUR BOSS

The starting point of an influential relationship with your boss is a clear understanding of your boss's goals and priorities, workplace concerns, and the pressures he or she is feeling. These are proxies for the *needs and interests* we encouraged you to understand with respect to your subordinates. They are the matters that absorb your boss's attention and, in some cases, create anxiety. You should be able to accurately answer these questions:

➢ What are your boss's goals and priorities?

➢ What knotty problem is he or she struggling with?

➢ What pressure, if any, is higher management putting on your boss?

➢ What accomplishment would make your boss a hero in the eyes of senior management?

➢ What kind of relationship does your boss have with his or her immediate superior? Is it tense? Collegial? Subservient?

If you can answer these questions, you'll be able to recognize things you can do—alone and through your own subordinates—to help your boss.

It's possible to identify your boss's main concerns through informal one-on-one meetings, staff meetings, lunches, and so forth. Like everyone else, bosses generally want to talk about the things that keep them awake at night *if* the people listening can be trusted. All they need to open up is an opportunity. So find occasions to talk with your boss about his or her concerns and priorities and how you can align your work with them. By doing this you will establish yourself in your boss's mind as a reliable and indispensable ally—like Cardinal Richelieu was to his king. That will enhance both your working relationship and your ability to influence this key person in your work life.

In this same vein, try to discover "no-go" areas. These are sensitive issues that your boss does *not* want to discuss or negotiate with you. Think of them as land mines to be avoided. Consider this example:

Helen joined the company six months ago as an assistant to the national sales manager. Always eager to improve operations and reduce costs, Helen believes that replacing the company's IT help desk with an outsourced service would be a great idea.

She is ready to spring her idea on her boss but decides to first run it past John, a long-term member of the department. "That's a good idea, Helen," he tells her. "But take my advice—don't bring it up."

"Why not?" she asks. "My numbers make sense, don't they?"

"Sure, they make sense," John replies. "But even though we are growing fast, this is still a family company at heart. Bill will never terminate folks until the wolf is at the door."

ADAPT TO YOUR BOSS'S WORK STYLE

Every boss has a preferred style for doing his or her work and dealing with subordinates like you. Do you know what that style is? If you learn your boss's preferences and adapt to them, your relationship will proceed smoothly and you'll be in a position to project influence.

Work style covers a number of areas:

➤ **Information Preferences.** Most bosses want to know about progress against deadlines, problems with important customers, new expenditures and revenue projections that may affect budget projections, and so forth. Talk to your superior about the specific matters on which he or she needs to be kept posted. You want to provide what is needed but not overload your boss with more than can be digested.

➤ **Information Format.** Different managers have different format preferences with respect to information. Some prefer a short, verbal report: "In a nutshell, tell me the current status of _____." Others want written reports with plenty of supporting data. Be careful using e-mail to inform your boss of key information unless he or she has requested it; many busy executives are woefully behind on checking their e-mails.

➤ **Time Demands.** How much time is your boss willing to give you? The typical subordinate wants more time with the boss than he or she is currently getting. But your boss may have other ideas. To maintain a good relationship, find a proper balance between your need for face time and your boss's ability or inclination to provide it.

➤ **Decision Making.** Managers spend a significant percentage of their time making decisions. Little ones: "What's the best time to schedule this year's performance appraisals?" Big ones: "Should we invest $13.5 million in a new enterprise software system or continue with the current system—or seek a third alternative?" Your boss's decision process represents a potential portal for your influence. A sound decision process involves (1) defining the problem or issue and its context, (2) creating a set of feasible alternatives, (3) objectively analyzing the alternatives, (4) choosing the best alternative, and (5) implementing the decision. Each of these steps represents an opportunity for you to contribute. Figure 5-1 offers tips on how you can influence your boss's decisions.

FIGURE 5-1. TIPS FOR INFLUENCING YOUR BOSS'S DECISIONS.

Understand how your boss makes decisions.	Ask yourself: Does your boss follow a rational process? Does your boss seek input from his or her people or go it alone?
Suggest alternatives.	Work with your boss and other knowledgeable parties to develop a set of at least three feasible alternative solutions.
Provide objective analysis of decision alternatives.	This is the "homework" step where a good subordinate can make a real contribution. Dig for the facts relative to each alternative. Identify the uncertainties.
Understand the political dimensions.	In organizations, every big decision has a political dimension. Find out what this dimension is and what its implications are for your boss.
Work out plans and a timetable for implementing the decision.	Making a good decision is only half the battle—implementation is equally important. This is another step in which a subordinate can make a major contribution. Ask for a meeting in which the two of you can plan the implementation of his or her decision.

. . . .

HOW TO *LOSE* INFLUENCE WITH YOUR BOSS

In tennis, amateur players generally defeat themselves by making mistakes: repeatedly hitting the ball out of bounds or into the net. People who seek to establish influence with their managers likewise defeat themselves by doing dumb things, such as the following:

> **Being a habitual bargainer when assignments are given.** Don't be a "What can you do for me?" person. Your boss will perceive dealings with you as a series of contests—which he or she doesn't have time for.

> **Upstaging.** Yes, it's nice to shine, but your job is to make your boss look good. Don't steal your boss's thunder—it will only create resentment and make you seem like a rival, not a trustworthy supporter.

> **Self-promoting.** It's fine to be ambitious, but instead of lobbying for attention or advancement, earn both through good work.

> **Failing to check in.** Keep your boss informed, even if it's only a quick update at the end of the day. Failure to inform will reduce trust in you.

. . . .

♦ ♦ ♦ ♦ ♦

Your boss has a tough job. The typical manager's day is fragmented with phone calls, meetings, people problems, and many fires to put out. There's seldom time to sit quietly, make plans, and think through the many decisions that must be made. The more order and support you can contribute to this chaotic situation, the greater the influence you will have.

CHAPTER REVIEW

To review what you have learned, take the following open-book review quiz.

1. Identify at least three attitudes that your boss must have in order for you to exert influence (e.g., he must "like you").

_____

_____

_____

2. To influence, you should understand and address the things that absorb your boss's attention. Besides the pressures put on your boss by higher management, what might those things be?

_____

_____

_____

_____

3. You'll be more influential with your boss if you understand and adapt to his or her preferred style for interacting with you. Name two aspects of a preferred work style as described in this chapter.

_____

_____

4. Identify one thing you can do to influence your boss's decisions.

_____

_____

_____

_____

NOTE

1. Sandy J. Wayne, Robert C. Liden, Isabel K. Graf, and Gerald R. Ferris, "The Role of Upward Influence Tactics in Human Resource Decisions," *Personnel Psychology* 50, no. 4 (published online December 7, 2006): 979–1006.

CHAPTER 6

THE ETHICS OF INFLUENCE

Our opening chapter defined influence as "a means of getting what we want *without* command or compulsion." As you've probably already concluded, this definition is broad enough to include a range of goals and methods, from unselfish and noble to manipulative and downright evil. For example, one person may use her influence to gain support for a program of change from which all will benefit, but another, fearing that a change in the status quo would undermine her position and privileges, may use her influence to block much-needed reform. In yet another case, a CEO may try to influence his board through the selective use of facts. He tells himself:

> I've explained all the benefits of my intended strategy to the
> board, but I've understated the downside risks. The
> company must change its strategy to stay competitive, but
> board members would never buy into my plans if they knew

the risks. Keeping the company alive and well is my responsibility, so I'll hedge the truth.

Each of these examples of influence has an ethical component.

Ethics is a term derived from the Greek word *ethos*, meaning "character" or "custom." It refers to a body of rules of conduct deemed acceptable by the larger community. Ethical behavior is that deemed "good" and "right" by the body of rules. In the workplace, ethical behavior includes:

- ➤ Being honest
- ➤ Showing respect for others
- ➤ Taking responsibility for one's actions
- ➤ Dealing fairly with fellow employees and other stakeholders
- ➤ Acknowledging the contributions of others
- ➤ Putting the legitimate goals of the organization first
- ➤ Showing compassion for those experiencing loss or misfortune

Workplace rules of acceptable and unacceptable behavior extend to the application of influence.

How do we know when our efforts to influence have crossed the line of ethical behavior? One way is to examine their ends and means. To be ethical, both the ends and the means of influence must satisfy standards of ethical behavior. Let's consider each.

ENDS

The first test of the ethical application of influence is to examine the intended end, or goal. History provides countless examples of people pursuing ethical and unethical goals. On the one hand, we have U.S. President Woodrow Wilson, who wore himself out trying to persuade the American public and Congress to support the establishment of a League of Nations, which he saw as a bulwark against a repeat of the horrors of World War I. On the other hand, we have Publius Claudius Pulcher, a disreputable and ambitious politico of the first century BCE, who sought to influence the Roman public to favor him and his sponsor, Julius Caesar. Claudius achieved his end by applying the principle of reciprocity to the Roman masses—in this case by distributing free grain at state expense. His goal was far from noble: Give Julius Caesar the public support he needed to usurp total power and dismantle the Roman Republic.

Consider the following characteristics of ethical and unethical workplace goals:

. . . .

ETHICAL GOALS (MUTUAL BENEFIT)	UNETHICAL GOALS (PURE SELF-INTEREST)
➤ Help the company achieve its legitimate goals.	➤ Do whatever is necessary to achieve one's personal goals, regardless of the impact on others and the organization.
➤ Persuade customers to purchase products or services that deliver what they promise.	➤ Persuade customers to purchase products and services, even those known to be dangerous, defective, or unsuitable.
➤ Influence coworkers to pursue actions or adopt attitudes that will make them successful.	➤ Influence coworkers to pursue actions or adopt attitudes that will damage their interests but advance one's own.

. . . .

We need only look to the business news to find examples of organizations and individuals applying influence in their pursuit of unethical goals. Consider these:

Insider trading in financial markets is illegal. It is also unethical, especially when insider executives use their influence with analysts and the business media to misrepresent the future prospects of their companies. Now-defunct Enron, whose shares rose to $90 on executive misrepresentations, provides a classic example. The company's managing director of investor relations obtained more than 18,000 shares of Enron stock for $15.51 a share and sold them for $49.77 per share a week *before* the public was told what she already knew: that Enron was facing huge losses.

Influencing customers through advertising to buy products known to be defective is a common area of unethical behavior. During the—1970s, Ford Motor Company produced a subcompact car it called the Pinto. A design flaw made the Pinto's fuel tank susceptible to puncture and ignition in a rear-end collision. The company knew of the problem, yet used its immense advertising establishment and millions in ad spending to sell tens of thousands of Pintos to the unknowing public. Twenty-one people were burned to death in Pinto collisions and many more were scarred for life. Subsequent lawsuits revealed a darker story: The company allegedly knew that it could remedy the problem for less than $11 per vehicle (1970s dollars), but it chose the payment of lawsuit damages as a cheaper alternative. In the end, the company escaped criminal charges but lost millions in compensatory and punitive damages. It also took a huge public relations hit, and its Pinto became known as "a barbeque that seats four."

Some cases of unethical goals involve pure individual self-interest masquerading under the guise of the organizational good. Consider the case of a growing company of 400 employees. It had long ago outsourced product fulfillment, which was deemed a non–core activity. However, a new vice president, Neal, lobbied for the reversal of this practice and for the construction of a product fulfillment center—under his management, of course. Using every ounce of his considerable power and persuasion, Neal eventually got his way, and the company spent millions building and staffing a new fulfillment center. People close to the situation knew the ugly truth: Neal's enthusiasm for the project had nothing to do with operational improvement and everything to do with the expansion of Neal's personal turf. With a capital improvement project, a larger budget, and the twenty-some employees of the fulfillment center reporting to him, Neal became a much bigger fish in the corporate pond. Neal's fulfillment center proved more costly and performed less ably than its outsourced predecessor.

The executive team was disappointed both with its decision and with Neal's self-serving behavior. Though he continued to wield organizational power, his influence decreased, and Neal was eventually forced out of the company. Still, it took the company more than ten years to reverse course on this costly decision.

Take a minute to examine your own applications of influence. What are your goals? Are they self-serving, or do they serve the interests of the company and/or those of your workplace colleagues and customers?

MEANS

Even when our ends are ethical, there are plenty of temptations to achieve them through unethical means: by cutting corners with the truth, by concealing and manipulating, by employing "the stick" when the carrot fails. Niccolò Machiavelli, author of the sixteenth-century treatise *The Prince,* stated what he saw as an irony: that good ends must often be achieved through evil deeds. In his view, ends justify the means:

> Anyone who would act up to a perfect standard of goodness in everything must be ruined among so many who are not good. It is essential therefore for a prince to have learnt how *to be other than good and to use, or not to use, his goodness as necessity requires.*[1] (Our italics for emphasis.)

Machiavelli's statement, of course, has associated his name ever since with an unflattering character "type." A Machiavellian person is one who will stoop to any means, including deception, violence, and manipulation, to achieve his ends. This is *not* something you should aspire to in your campaign to have greater workplace influence. Applying influence in unethical ways may bring success in the short term, but it will hurt you in the end. Consider the following ethical and unethical means:

· ·

ETHICAL MEANS (HONEST DEALINGS)	UNETHICAL MEANS (LYING OR MISREPRESENTING FACTS)
➢ Disclosing one's agenda or interests	➢ Concealing or misrepresenting one's agenda or interests

- Delivering information that reflects both sides of an issue

- Delivering information that supports one's interest while withholding unfavorable information

- Ensuring transparency

- Manipulating and dissembling

- Promising only what one can deliver

- Promising more than what one can deliver

. . . .

Consider this example of ethical means at work:

Janet works as a representative for a major stockbrokerage firm. The company's analysts have just issued a report and "buy" recommendation on XYZ Technology. Believing that her client, Mrs. Jones, would benefit by owning XYZ shares, Janet gives her a call.

"Hello, Mrs. Jones. This is Janet calling. I wanted you to know about our company's report on XYZ Technology. Our analysts think it's a good buy and I believe it would fit well in your current portfolio."

"Okay," Mrs. Jones responds. "Tell me about this company."

"I will," says Janet. "But before I do, in the spirit of full disclosure, I want you to know that my company does investment banking work for XYZ."

Janet then tells her client about XYZ and its potential for growth and recommends a purchase of 500 shares for her client's portfolio.

In this case, the banking relationship between XYZ Technology and Janet's company represented a *potential* conflict of interest. By disclosing this relationship *before* encouraging Mrs. Jones to make a purchase, Janet did the ethical thing. Here's another example:

> Sam, a product manager for an optical instruments company, is meeting with the executive team to discuss possible development of a new generation of telescopes for amateur astronomers. Sam was asked to study the market and to explore potential avenues for upgrading the company's telescopic offerings.
>
> Sam gives each member his written report, then proceeds with a stand-up presentation. He explains that he found three credible alternative approaches: (1) incremental improvement to the existing product line, (2) the addition of computer control technology to the entire line, and (3) development of an entirely new product generation based on a revolutionary new compact optical design. Sam highly favors the third alternative and is prepared to argue in its favor. But he sees his first duty to the executive team as evenhandedly presenting the facts, and the pros and cons of *each* alternative—which he does.

A less ethical Sam would not have been so evenhanded. Instead, he would have presented only the facts that favored his preferred alternative. Advocacy of that type would have denied the executive team the full range of information it needed to make a good decision. There is a time for advocacy, but it should not take place until all the facts have been laid on the table, especially when others trust in your objectivity and evenhandedness. The type of objectivity that Sam exemplifies in this case will earn him even more trust and influence. A person who conceals all but the most favorable information is eventually found out, losing trust and influence.

We needn't look far in the world of commerce to spot instances of unethical means:

> With growing public awareness of the ill effects of trans fats in food, a snack food manufacturer is prominently labeling certain products as having no trans fats, which is true, even though the products in question are loaded with high levels of other fats and additives. Buyers have to read the fine print to find the truth. By playing up "no trans fats," the company is aiming to persuade customers that they are buying a healthy product, even though they are not.
>
> Jack meets with his direct reports in the marketing department every Monday morning. He tosses out ideas and tentative plans and then solicits his subordinates' responses and suggestions. At first, Jack's staff members appreciate his willingness to involve them in his plans and decisions, but it soon becomes clear that their suggestions are never adopted. One person puts it this way: "Jack is a manipulator. He tries to give the appearance that our ideas matter, but that's just a cover. In the end, he does exactly what he intended to do all along."

Does your company misrepresent the truth to customers or employees, as the snack food company is clearly doing? Do you know manipulators like Jack? Both are bound to lose influence when their unethical behaviors are revealed.

◆ ◆ ◆ ◆ ◆

We've stated before that it takes a long time to build personal influence. Influence is, in fact, a work in progress. People observe what you do and listen to what you say. Every observation adds one more impression of the kind of person you are at bottom. Do you pursue ethical goals? Are you ethical in your behavior toward others? Cumulative impressions of you will, over time, determine how open others will be to your influence. However, one major ethical lapse can neutralize your influence in a heartbeat.

CHAPTER REVIEW

To review what you have learned, take the following open-book review quiz.

1. Ethics refers to a body of rules of conduct deemed acceptable by the larger community. Name at least three ethical behaviors cited in this chapter.

_____

_____

_____

_____

2. Provide an example of an ethical and an unethical workplace goal.

_____

_____

_____

_____

3. Provide a workplace example of an ethical and an unethical means.

_____

_____

_____

_____

NOTE

1. Niccolò Machiavelli, *The Prince*, The Harvard Classics, Charles W. Elliot, ed. (New York: P.F. Collier & Sons, 1910), 53.

GLOSSARY

Aggression

A mode of behavior or communication in which a person has no reluctance to impose his or her views on others, or harm their interests in the pursuit of his or her own. Rather than collaborate with others, the aggressive person prefers to dominate them, using threats, organizational authority, or bullying when necessary.

Assertiveness

A mode of personal behavior and communication characterized by a willingness to stand up for one's needs and interests in an open and direct way.

Command-and-control

A model of management in which information relative to customers and operations flows upward through the chain of command. Decisions are made at the top, then communicated downward through the same chain for execution.

Community of interest

A group of people who share common concerns or interests. A group of this type typically meets periodically to share ideas, information, and best-practice solutions for common concerns.

Employee empowerment

A management model that gives subordinates substantial discretion in how they accomplish their objectives.

Ethics

A body of rules of conduct deemed acceptable by the larger community.

Favor effect

The likelihood that a person whom you've asked for a favor will, once he or she has complied, be positively disposed to you and will likely be willing to do you another favor.

Frame

A mental window through which we view reality.

Influence

A means of getting what we want *without* command or compulsion.

Influence map

A graphic representation of the patterns and strength of influence.

Passivity

An unassertive condition characterized by submissiveness and a fear of standing up for one's needs and interests or an unwillingness to do so.

Peer

A person of roughly equal organizational standing over whom one has no authority.

Peer influence (or peer pressure)

The influence that group values and behaviors exert on individuals.

Persuasion

A process of communication through which one person alters the beliefs, attitudes, or actions of others. This process uses rhetorical tools such as structured language, logical argument, and emotional appeals.

Power

The ability to get what we want by virtue of command or compulsion.

Principle of reciprocity

A principle that asserts that a favor done for someone demands a favor in return.

Self-actualization

In Maslow's hierarchy of human needs, the feeling people have when they are in control of their lives, and when they sense that they are exploiting their full potential.

Silo mentality

The narrowness of focus and outlook caused by work within specialized functional units. In the worst cases, people within silos become so insular that they lose sight of the organization's goals and substitute self-interest in their place.

Thought leader

A person to whom others turn for advice or new ideas.

SELECTED READING

Cialdini, Robert B. "Harnessing the Science of Persuasion." *Harvard Business Review* (October 2001).

Cohen, Allan R., and David L. Bradford. *Influence Without Authority.* New York: John Wiley & Sons, 1991.

Griskevicious, Vladas, Robert B. Cialdini, and Noah J. Goldstein. "Applying (and Resisting) Peer Influence." *MIT Sloan Management Review* 49, no. 2 (Winter 2008).

Patterson, Kerry, Joseph Grenny, David Maxfield, Ron McMillan, and Al Switzler. *Influencer: The Power to Change Anything.* New York: McGraw Hill, 2007.

Pfeffer, Jeffrey. *Managing with Power: Politics and Influence in Organizations.* Boston: Harvard Business School Press, 1994.

INDEX